Contents

Foreword

"The time has arrived; the kingdom of God is upon you. Repent, and believe the gospel."

"Strive to enter through the narrow door; for many, I tell you, will try to enter and will not be able. When once the owner of the house has got up and shut the door, and you begin to stand outside and to knock at the door, saying, 'Lord, open to us,' then in reply he will say to you, 'I do not know where you come from.' Then you will begin to say, 'We ate and drank with you, and you taught in our streets.' But he will say, 'I do not know where you come from; go away from me, all you evildoers!'"

"I came into the world as light, so that everyone who believes in me might not remain in darkness. And if anyone hears my words and does not observe them, I do not condemn him, for I did not come to condemn the world but to save the world. Whoever rejects me and does not accept my words has something to judge him: the word that I spoke, it will condemn him on the last day, because I did not speak on my own, but the Father who sent me commanded me what to say and speak. And I know that his commandment is eternal life."

"Therefore, everyone who listens to these words of mine and acts on them will be like a sensible man who built his house on rock. Rain came down, floods rose, gales blew and hurled themselves against that house, and it did not fall: it was founded on rock. But everyone who listens to these words of mine and does not act on them will be like a stupid man who built his house on sand. Rain came down, floods rose, gales blew and struck that house, and it fell; and what a fall it had!"

Jesus,
Son of God,
Son of Mary.

1. Mark 1:15   Revised English Bible (REB)
2. Luke 13:24–27   New Revised Standard Version of
                    the Bible (NRSV)
3. John 12:46–50   New American Bible (NAB)
4. Matthew 7:24–27 New Jerusalem Bible (NJB)

Introduction

> Jesus said to him, "You must love the Lord your
> God with all your heart, with all your soul, and
> with all your mind. This is the greatest and the
> first commandment."
>
> (Mt 22:37–38, NJB)

"Jesus said" – let this phrase signify what the inspired
writers of the four Gospels intended it to signify. All the
sayings quoted in this book are ascribed to Jesus by
these evangelists.

"Heart," "soul," "mind" – Jesus is emphasizing this:
you must love the Lord with all your faculties, with all
your resources, with your entire being. It is the greatest
thing you can do. It must come first.

How does Our Lord want us to love him? The answer
is found in the Gospel according to John, Chapter
Fourteen. Jesus declares, "If you love me you will obey
my commands" (v. 15, REB). Again, in verse 21 (NJB),
"Whoever holds to my commandments and keeps them
is the one who loves me." And still again, "Whoever
loves me will keep my word" (v. 23, NAB).

This is the way Jesus wishes to be loved: that we obey
his commands. The person who genuinely loves Jesus
adheres to his word. Conversely, he who keeps Jesus'
commandments – that is, in spirit and in truth, and not

by merely going through the motions – demonstrates his love for him.

Do not look upon a commandment as an irksome encumbrance. Once you decide to live it, you will discover that Jesus is right when he says, "Yes, my yoke is easy and my burden light" (Mt 11:30, NJB). Living Jesus' commands brings understanding and freedom. He promised, "If you remain in my word, you will truly be my disciples, and you will know the truth, and the truth will set you free" (Jn 8:31–32, NAB).

Besides being an order, a commandment is also a guide and an invitation. For example, when Jesus tells you to forgive an enemy, he is showing you a very effective way of handling a difficult situation. At the same time, he is inviting you to love your enemy and himself, through the act of forgiveness.

Love of Jesus should be an indispensable attribute of all Christians, especially the leaders. Jesus made sure that Peter understood this:

> After breakfast Jesus said to Simon Peter, "Simon son of John, do you love me more than these others?" "Yes, Lord," he answered, "you know that I love you." "Then feed my lambs," he said. A second time he asked, "Simon son of John, do you love me?" "Yes, Lord, you know I love you." "Then tend my sheep." A third time he said, "Simon son of John, do you love me?" Peter was hurt that he asked him a third time, "Do you love me?" "Lord," he said, "you know everything; you

know I love you." Jesus said, "Then feed my sheep."

(Jn 21:15–17, REB)

Jesus makes three promises to those who love him. The first is this: "Whoever loves me will keep my word, and my Father will love him, and we will come to him and make our dwelling with him" (Jn 14:23, NAB). When you obey Jesus, God the Father loves you. Both he and Jesus will enter your heart and stay there. They will never say to you, "I do not know where you come from; go away from me." For you there will be no rejection, no condemnation on the last day. Against you the door to the Kingdom will not be shut. Your house is built on a firm foundation; it will not fall.

The second promise is: "Whoever holds to my commandments and keeps them is the one who loves me; and whoever loves me will be loved by my Father, and I shall love him and reveal myself to him" (Jn 14:21, NJB). Besides the Father's love you will also receive that of Jesus. You will come to know him much more, for he will disclose himself to you, imparting to you his thoughts, and teaching you his ways. In you light will exist, not darkness.

The third promise is: "If you love me you will obey my commands; and I will ask the Father, and he will give you another to be your advocate, who will be with you for ever – the Spirit of truth" (Jn 14:15–17, REB). The word *advocate* is translated from the Greek *parakletos*. A "parakletos" is a defence lawyer. But *the Parakletos*, the Holy Spirit, is more than just that. Whereas a lawyer

may act on your behalf in one case and only on a professional basis, the Holy Spirit is always lovingly and passionately on your side. He is committed totally to your present and eternal well-being. He has been called out to speak and intercede for you, to teach and advise you, to console, protect, defend, and fight for you. He witnesses to Jesus and the truth of his teachings; he gives evidence against the lies of the world; he confers strength and courage, and provides a shield and security in your walk with the Lord. And this Counsellor and Comforter will be given to you and will remain with you for ever because of your obedience to Jesus.

If you love God, if you keep his commandments, the Father, Jesus, and the Holy Spirit are all present in you, with their love, their friendship, their acceptance, their wisdom, their power.

Listen to Jesus – his Father commands it (Lk 9:35). Do whatever he tells you – his mother requests it (Jn 2:5). Put him in the first place in your life; keep him at the centre of your being. Make sure, if he should ask you in a little while, "Simon son of John, do you love me? Andrew son of George, do you love me? Mary daughter of Joan, do you love me?" that you can answer with conviction, with honesty, with heartfelt insistence, "Lord, you know everything; you know that I love you."

Let him know! Let him know!

SECTION

I

LOVE

LOVE

Part 1

We have just seen that love of Jesus involves carrying out what he commands. We invite you, dear reader, to spend some quality time familiarizing yourself with his teachings. But do not do this for the sake of discussion or commentary. We beg you to take Jesus' gospel to heart, and live it.

Let us begin with two suggestions. First, when meditating on the gospel readings provided, be sure to apply them to yourself, not to anybody else. Do not use them to judge others.

Second, apply the readings in a positive way. If you find that Jesus' teachings challenge your lifestyle, do not give in to thoughts like: "The gospel may be fine for some people, but don't bother me with it. I am busy with more important matters. Religion should not interfere with my private affairs anyway." Or, "Lots of men and women never read the Bible; they don't even go to church. Why should I have to do more?" Or, "I admit that I'm not a perfect Christian. But it's so bothersome

to change. If adjustments had been introduced earlier in my youth it might have made a difference. It is too late now; I'll simply carry on as before."

Think along these lines instead: "I will open my heart to Jesus. He knows it takes most people repeated prodding over the years before they learn what he wants them to learn. But he has allowed for that. He does not condemn me for the lost chances. He will help me. His way will make me a much better individual. By becoming better, I will benefit myself and all those around me. Even if these are my last days on earth, it is not useless to start. The good that comes from my transformation will, at the very least, be an enormous influence on my loved ones."

The following is a rough example of how to use the gospel passages. Reading Two opens with the command: "But I say to you that listen, Love your enemies, do good to those who hate you, bless those who curse you, pray for those who abuse you." Call to mind an enemy. If you do not have one, think of a person you dislike or do not get along with, or against whom you bear a grudge or feel resentment. If there are several, begin by picking a comparably less troublesome one. He or she is probably somebody in your home or at your place of work. (See the list on page 123.)

"Love your enemies." Decide to love this person from now on. Do not just promise to do it, but actually act lovingly towards him. "Do good to those who hate you." Plan right away a good deed you will do for him. "Bless those who curse you." From this day forward say only what is good about this person. Stop gossiping about

him. Look for admirable qualities in him. Make it a point to talk nicely to him, perhaps with genuine compliments and words of encouragement. Do not be unkind again. "Pray for those who abuse you." Stop reading for a moment. Pray for this person immediately. Ask God to bestow his choicest graces upon him.

"If anyone strikes you on the cheek, offer the other also." People may not go about physically slapping each other across the face, but they often do so with stinging remarks. If this person insults you, do not insult him back. If he goes a step further by getting angry at you, let him! "From anyone who takes away your coat do not withhold even your shirt."

"Give to everyone who begs from you." Should this person request something legitimate, do not spite him by outright refusal. Give him what he asks. Even if you are not able to comply, at least pass on information as to how he might find it elsewhere.

"And if anyone takes away your goods, do not ask for them again." Should he misappropriate what belongs to you and not return it, be quietly gracious.

And if you have been insistent that any reconciliation among you must come from his side, perhaps you can initiate the first move yourself. "Do to others as you would have them do to you."

"If you love those who love you, what credit is that to you? For even sinners love those who love them. If you do good to those who do good to you, what credit is that to you? For even sinners do the same. If you lend to those from whom you hope to receive, what credit is that to you? Even sinners lend to sinners, to receive as much

again. But love your enemies, do good, and lend, expecting nothing in return. Your reward will be great." It is in loving this person who has no love for you, in doing good to him who may not return the favour, in lending to him who may never reimburse you – it is in living this way that you will be extraordinarily compensated. Your generosity may eventually smooth out the hostilities between the two of you; you may gain an excellent friend; you may win a new disciple for Christ; your own soul will be made cleaner; and you will show yourself to be a child of God.

"You will be children of the Most High; for he is kind to the ungrateful and the wicked." This person with whom you seek to make peace is often ungrateful, and wicked as well. God is kind to him and forgives him. Will you also be kind to him? Will you also forgive him?

Prayer

"This is how you should pray:

Our Father in heaven,
may your name be hallowed;
your kingdom come,
your will be done,
on earth as in heaven.
Give us today our daily bread.
Forgive us the wrong we have done,
as we have forgiven those who have wronged us.
And do not put us to the test,
but save us from the evil one.

"For if you forgive others the wrongs they have done,
your heavenly Father will also forgive you; but if you do
not forgive others, then your Father will not forgive the
wrongs that you have done" (Mt 6:9–15, REB).

Listen to Jesus now. Take as long as you wish to
meditate on the following readings.

Reading One

"Love the Lord your God with all your heart, with all your soul, and with all your mind." That is the greatest, the first commandment. The second is like it: "Love your neighbour as yourself." Everything in the law and the prophets hangs on these two commandments.

Anyone who has received my commands and obeys them – he it is who loves me; and he who loves me will be loved by my Father; and I will love him and disclose myself to him.

When the Son of Man comes in his glory and all the angels with him, he will sit on his glorious throne, with all the nations gathered before him. He will separate people into two groups, as a shepherd separates the sheep from the goats; he will place the sheep on his right hand and the goats on his left. Then the king will say to those on his right, "You have my Father's blessing; come, take possession of the kingdom that has been ready for you since the world was made. For when I was hungry, you gave me food; when thirsty, you gave me drink; when I was a stranger, you took me into your home; when naked, you clothed me; when I was ill, you came to my help; when in prison, you visited me." Then the righteous will reply, "Lord, when was it that we saw you hungry and fed you, or thirsty and gave you drink, a stranger and took you home, or naked and clothed you? When did we see you ill or in prison, and came to visit

you?" And the king will answer, "Truly I tell you: anything you did for one of my brothers here, however insignificant, you did for me."

I have spoken thus to you, so that my joy may be in you, and your joy complete. This is my commandment: love one another, as I have loved you.

If there is this love among you, then everyone will know that you are my disciples.

1. Mt 22:37–40. 2. Jn 14:21. 3. Mt 25:31–40. 4. Jn 15:11–12. 5. Jn 13:35. (REB)

*

Reading Two

But I say to you that listen, Love your enemies, do good to those who hate you, bless those who curse you, pray for those who abuse you. If anyone strikes you on the cheek, offer the other also; and from anyone who takes away your coat, do not withhold even your shirt. Give to everyone who begs from you; and if anyone takes away your goods, do not ask for them again. Do to others as you would have them do to you.

  If you love those who love you, what credit is that to you? For even sinners love those who love them. If you do good to those who do good to you, what credit is that to you? For even sinners do the same. If you lend to those from whom you hope to receive, what credit is that

to you? Even sinners lend to sinners, to receive as much again. But love your enemies, do good, and lend, expecting nothing in return. Your reward will be great, and you will be children of the Most High; for he is kind to the ungrateful and the wicked.

Give, and it will be given to you. A good measure, pressed down, shaken together, running over, will be put into your lap; for the measure you give will be the measure you get back.

1. Lk 6:27–35. 2. Lk 6:38. (NRSV)

*

Reading Three

That is why the kingdom of heaven may be likened to a king who decided to settle accounts with his servants. When he began the accounting, a debtor was brought before him who owed him a huge amount. Since he had no way of paying it back, his master ordered him to be sold, along with his wife, his children, and all his property, in payment of the debt. At that, the servant fell down, did him homage, and said, "Be patient with me, and I will pay you back in full." Moved with compassion the master of that servant let him go and forgave him the loan. When that servant had left, he found one of his fellow servants who owed him a much smaller amount. He seized him and started to choke him, demanding, "Pay back what you owe." Falling to his knees, his

fellow servant begged him, "Be patient with me, and I will pay you back." But he refused. Instead, he had him put in prison until he paid back the debt. Now when his fellow servants saw what had happened, they were deeply disturbed, and went to their master and reported the whole affair. His master summoned him and said to him, "You wicked servant! I forgave you your entire debt because you begged me to. Should you not have had pity on your fellow servant, as I had pity on you?" Then in anger his master handed him over to the torturers until he should pay back the whole debt. So will my heavenly Father do to you, unless each of you forgives his brother from his heart.

1. Mt 18:23–35. (NAB)

*

Reading Four

Always treat others as you would like them to treat you: that is the law and the prophets.

If your brother does wrong, reprove him; and if he repents, forgive him. Even if he wrongs you seven times in a day and comes back to you seven times saying, "I am sorry," you are to forgive him.

It is not the healthy who need a doctor, but the sick. Go and learn what this text means, "I require mercy, not sacrifice."

Be compassionate, as your Father is compassionate.

1. Mt 7:12. 2. Lk 17:3–4. 3. Mt 9:12–13. 4. Lk 6:36.
(REB)

LOVE

Part 2

Let us review briefly. In Reading One Jesus says, "Love the Lord your God with all your heart, with all your soul, and with all your mind." How does Our Lord want us to love him? "Anyone who has received my commands and obeys them – he it is who loves me." And what does he command? "This is my commandment: love one another, as I have loved you."

When we love each other we are obeying Jesus, and in obeying we show our love for him in the same action. That is a small reason why he says, "Truly I tell you: anything you did for one of my brothers here, however insignificant, you did for me."

In obedience to Jesus, and in union with him, feed the hungry and give drink to the thirsty. Do it personally or with monetary contributions. In whatever capacity you can, shelter the homeless, clothe the naked, look after the sick, visit the confined. Drop in to see the elderly. Bring them a present. Telephone the bedridden, the housebound, those with no friends. Give alms to the

poor. Pray for all in need. Open your heart to orphans and widows. Speak to the young. Spend time with your adolescents. There are people who hunger and thirst because no one cares for them.

In the second reading Jesus tells us to love our enemies. We have already seen how the passage can be used to heal the divisions between us and the people with whom we are experiencing problems. Of course, no passage has to be applied in the way suggested in this book. When Jesus says, "Give to everyone who begs from you," the "everyone" does not refer only to enemies or persons we do not like.

In the next paragraph he says, "Give, and it will be given to you." Give and God will shower his favours on you most generously. How generously? Imagine yourself buying potatoes from a kind-hearted farmer. Selling by the basket and not by weight, this good man fills your container to the very top. Not satisfied with that, he proceeds to shake it, eliminating many of the air spaces. He then presses the potatoes together tightly and adds more, till the basket overflows. That is how unstintingly God will reward you. For he says, "Give, and it will be given to you. A good measure, pressed down, shaken together, running over, will be put into your lap."

In Reading Three, the theme of forgiveness is accentuated by a parable. As God has forgiven you for much greater sins, forgive now your spouse who has wronged you, though many times, still, only in very small ways. Forgive your relatives, your friends, your colleagues. Blot out their offences from your memory

forever. Pray for them and be good to them from this moment on.

In the fourth reading we are asked to be "compassionate, as your Father is compassionate." The word *compassion* is made up of the prefix *com*, which means 'with,' and the Latin *pati (passus)* meaning 'to suffer or feel.' To be compassionate means to be able to identify with the sufferings and feelings of another. The sense of the word includes one's willingness to help.

That brings us to the next group of teachings. Reading Five is from the Prodigal Son parable. "There was a man who had two sons. The younger of them said to his father, 'Father, give me the share of property that will belong to me.' So he divided his property between them. A few days later the younger son gathered all he had and traveled to a distant country, and there he squandered his property in dissolute living." You know the rest of the story. In the midst of a famine, the destitute lad decided to go home. "But while he was still far off, his father saw him and was *filled with compassion*." Compassion! He sympathized with the son's feelings and sufferings. He understood his son's immaturity and lack of discipline. He knew how young people could make mistakes. He recognized human sinfulness. But the boy had now repented. He had returned. Instead of condemning his son, the father "ran and put his arms around him and kissed him."

One very important thing to remember about this parable is who it was that related it. Jesus did! Jesus knew about people who squandered their lives in dissolute living. He saw what human beings could

become. He was well aware of sin and those who committed them. He told the story to highlight his Father's unswerving love for his children.

He said, "Which one of you, having a hundred sheep and losing one of them, does not leave the ninety-nine in the wilderness and go after the one that is lost until he finds it? When he has found it, he lays it on his shoulders and rejoices. And when he comes home, he calls together his friends and neighbors, saying to them, 'Rejoice with me, for I have found my sheep that was lost.' Just so, I tell you, there will be more joy in heaven over one sinner who repents than over ninety-nine righteous persons who need no repentance" (Lk 15:4–7, NRSV).

If you have led a life of sinfulness, bear in mind that God has not given up on you. He looks for you lovingly because he cares about your eternal happiness. He will not stop until he finds you. In the company of his angels he will celebrate your homecoming with great jubilation.

The parable in Reading Six illustrates God's generosity towards his people. Jesus introduces it with these words: "The kingdom of Heaven is like this." There was a landowner who started hiring workers for his vineyard in the morning. At intervals during the day he invited more people. "An hour before sunset he went out and found another group standing there; so he said to them, 'Why are you standing here all day doing nothing?' 'Because no one has hired us,' they replied; so he told them, 'Go and join the others in the vineyard.'" And, like those who came in earlier, the latecomers were then paid the full day's wages!

Reading Seven begins with this warning: "Take care that you do not despise one of these little ones." "Little ones" does not refer only to children. Little ones are also people that we tend to look down on for any number of reasons. For example, we may scorn their opinions on certain matters; we may disdain their physical appearance, their psychological immaturity, their manners… As we ponder this reading, we should bring to mind the people we ignore, the ones we ridicule or curse, those we disparage – face to face or behind their backs. Remember also those to whom we often exhibit an expression that says, "I am irritated by your presence; I am too occupied to speak to you; you are not fit to carry on a meaningful relationship with me." (See the list on page 123.) In addition, remember those in our families, and those who hold positions below us in our places of work, especially the ones we nag, or scream at, or order around.

In this reading Jesus also says, "Do not judge, so that you may not be judged." The word "judged" at the end of the sentence refers to God's just judgement on the last day. But the third word, "judge", means, in this context, censure, find fault, blame, condemn. Many people today delight in complaining, mocking, sneering at things they do not understand, and making pronouncements on every topic that comes up in conversation. The more they can find to criticize, the bigger they regard themselves. Much of their idle talk is devoted to putting others down and puffing themselves up. They constantly overrate themselves but hastily undervalue others. They take immense pleasure in wishing misfortune on those

they deplore so as to justify their verbal abuse. Blind to their own ill-will, they spread nasty rumours about the people whose shortcomings they think they see. Instead of helping their neighbours to improve and praying for them, they fan the flame of hatred by inciting derision and hostility. Their speech reveals the wickedness inside. As Jesus says, "Vipers' brood! How can your words be good when you yourselves are evil? It is from the fullness of the heart that the mouth speaks. Good people from their store of good produce good; and evil people from their store of evil produce evil. I tell you this: every thoughtless word you speak you will have to account for on the day of judgement. For out of your own mouth you will be acquitted; out of your own mouth you will be condemned" (Mt 12:34–37, REB).

Do not be like that. It is not love.

The eighth reading deals with humility. "Whoever wishes to be great among you must be your servant, and whoever wishes to be first among you must be your slave." "For all who exalt themselves will be humbled, but all who humble themselves will be exalted." Great persons are not the ones who look to be admired and to be treated with extra courtesy everywhere they go. Great persons are those who serve quietly in humility and love.

Reading Nine ends Section I. Here, we have a narrative: Jesus waits on his apostles at the Last Supper by washing their feet. After the washing he says, "You call me Master and Lord, and rightly; so I am. If I, then, the Lord and Master, have washed your feet, you must wash each other's feet." Jesus is telling us to attend to one another in small kindnesses. Love does not consist

in grandiose deeds. Love lies in ministering to those who are near. We can perform tasks like cleaning the dishes for our family after a meal. We can take out the garbage even though it is not our customary duty to do so. We can make someone a cup of coffee or tea. We can offer to help an acquaintance who is busy or sick. These are the kinds of things Jesus means primarily when he speaks about serving, not the more visible or supposedly more exalted undertakings that some public figures are engaged in.

When we meditate on Jesus' teachings, we may discover we are not as good at being Christians as we thought. We are, in fact, quite sinful. Keep in mind, however, the suggestion made at the outset: we must not apply these readings negatively. Jesus certainly wants us not to fall into sin at all, but if we do, he gives us the opportunity to repent, as in the case of the Prodigal Son who came home saying, "Father, I have sinned against heaven and before you; I am no longer worthy to be called your son."

If we really resolve to change for the better, we can count on God's forgiveness and mercy. Look at how the father in the parable responded to his penitent son. "But the father said to his slaves, 'Quickly, bring out a robe – the best one – and put it on him; put a ring on his finger and sandals on his feet.'" We can expect our Father to welcome us similarly. He will let us wear his best robe to remind us that we have been created to be images of himself. We can expect him to give us his ring, to show that we are members of the family, we are his daughters and sons, we are his heirs. He will put shoes on our feet,

letting us know he does not want us roaming about like barefooted orphans, that he wants to take care of us, that we should come to him for all our needs. We can expect him to say to his servants, "… let us eat and celebrate; for this son of mine was dead and is alive again; he was lost and is found." He does not dwell on the painful memory that we were once dead and lost. He is ecstatically delighted that we are alive and reunited with him safe and sound.

Our Father is compassionate. He is forgiving. He is generous. He sent Jesus to tell the wayward, "I did not come to call the virtuous, but sinners" (Mt 9:13, REB). It is not good to be always negative, but it is also wrong to habitually gloss over Jesus' teachings and say, "His words are not about me. I am a decent enough person." Rather, it is proper to admit our sinfulness. Sinners are the people Jesus came to call.

And, perhaps, after we have heeded his call, we could move forward and become more loving and less self-centred for the blessing of others. We could take it upon ourselves to pray and work for the conversion of all transgressors, that they, too, would turn back to God and be received into the happiness of his kingdom forever.

Jesus said, "I have spoken thus to you, so that my joy may be in you, and *your joy* complete. This is my commandment: love one another, as I have loved you" (Jn 15:11–12, REB). Jesus did not give commandments to make our lives difficult. He wants us to love each other so that true joy will come into us. That is precisely the purpose of his teachings – our joy. If we extend our love to relatives and friends, to enemies, and to the least

of Jesus' brothers and sisters, his joy will become ours, and his love and peace will flow out from us to all his people, especially to those with whom we come in contact each and every day.

Prayer

God, you are infinitely superior to me, yet you love me so humbly and persistently.
May I learn to love my neighbours as you love me, no matter how inferior I imagine them to be.
May I remember that you love them also,
that they too are created for everlasting glory in Heaven.
When difficulties arise with anyone, let me always turn to you first.
Your Spirit brings understanding, and peace.

Now, listen to Jesus. Concentrate on his words and not on these sketchy introductory remarks. Spend more time on Reading Seven, paying special attention to the passage about the speck and the log.

Reading Five

There was a man who had two sons. The younger of them said to his father, "Father, give me the share of property that will belong to me." So he divided his property between them. A few days later the younger son gathered all he had and traveled to a distant country, and there he squandered his property in dissolute living. When he had spent everything, a severe famine took place throughout that country, and he began to be in need. So he went and hired himself out to one of the citizens of that country, who sent him to his fields to feed pigs. He would gladly have filled himself with the pods that the pigs were eating; and no one gave him anything. But when he came to himself he said, "How many of my father's hired hands have bread enough and to spare, but here I am dying of hunger! I will get up and go to my father, and I will say to him, 'Father, I have sinned against heaven and before you; I am no longer worthy to be called your son; treat me like one of your hired hands.'" So he set off and went to his father. But while he was still far off, his father saw him and was filled with compassion; he ran and put his arms around him and kissed him. Then the son said to him, "Father, I have sinned against heaven and before you; I am no longer worthy to be called your son." But the father said to his slaves, "Quickly, bring out a robe – the best one – and put it on him; put a ring on his finger and sandals on his feet. And get the fatted calf and kill it, and let us eat

and celebrate; for this son of mine was dead and is alive again; he was lost and is found."

1. Lk 15:11–24. (NRSV)

*

Reading Six

All that the Father gives me will come to me, and anyone who comes to me I will never turn away. I have come down from heaven, to do not my own will, but the will of him who sent me. It is his will that I should not lose even one of those that he has given me, but should raise them all up on the last day. For it is my Father's will that everyone who sees the Son and has faith in him should have eternal life; and I will raise them up on the last day.

The kingdom of Heaven is like this. There was once a landowner who went out early one morning to hire labourers for his vineyard; and after agreeing to pay them the usual day's wage he sent them off to work. Three hours later he went out again and saw some more men standing idle in the market-place. "Go and join the others in the vineyard," he said, "and I will pay you a fair wage"; so off they went. At midday he went out again, and at three in the afternoon, and made the same arrangement as before. An hour before sunset he went out and found another group standing there; so he said to them, "Why are you standing here all day doing

nothing?" "Because no one has hired us," they replied; so he told them, "Go and join the others in the vineyard." When evening fell, the owner of the vineyard said to the overseer, "Call the labourers and give them their pay, beginning with those who came last and ending with the first." Those who had started work an hour before sunset came forward, and were paid the full day's wage.

I have come that they may have life, and may have it in all its fullness.

1. Jn 6:37–40. 2. Mt 20:1–9. 3. Jn 10:10. (REB)

*

Reading Seven

Take care that you do not despise one of these little ones; for, I tell you, in heaven their angels continually see the face of my Father in heaven.

You have heard that it was said to those of ancient times, "You shall not murder"; and "whoever murders shall be liable to judgment." But I say to you that if you are angry with a brother or sister, you will be liable to judgment; and if you insult a brother or sister, you will be liable to the council; and if you say, "You fool," you will be liable to the hell of fire.

Do not judge, so that you may not be judged. For with the judgment you make you will be judged, and the measure you give will be the measure you get. Why do you see the speck in your neighbor's eye, but do not notice the log in your own eye? Or how can you say to your neighbor, "Let me take the speck out of your eye," while the log is in your own eye? You hypocrite, first take the log out of your own eye, and then you will see clearly to take the speck out of your neighbor's eye.

Do not judge, and you will not be judged; do not condemn, and you will not be condemned. Forgive, and you will be forgiven.

1. Mt 18:10. 2. Mt 5:21–22. 3. Mt 7:1–5. 4. Lk 6:37. (NRSV)

*

Reading Eight

Truly I tell you, unless you change and become like children, you will never enter the kingdom of heaven. Whoever becomes humble like this child is the greatest in the kingdom of heaven.

Two men went up to the temple to pray, one a Pharisee and the other a tax collector. The Pharisee, standing by himself, was praying thus, "God, I thank you that I am not like other people: thieves, rogues, adulterers, or even like this tax collector. I fast twice a week; I give a tenth

of all my income." But the tax collector, standing far off, would not even look up to heaven, but was beating his breast and saying, "God, be merciful to me, a sinner!" I tell you, this man went down to his home justified rather than the other; for all who exalt themselves will be humbled, but all who humble themselves will be exalted.

Who among you would say to your slave who has just come in from plowing or tending sheep in the field, "Come here at once and take your place at the table"? Would you not rather say to him, "Prepare supper for me, put on your apron and serve me while I eat and drink; later you may eat and drink"? Do you thank the slave for doing what was commanded? So you also, when you have done all that you were ordered to do, say, "We are worthless slaves; we have done only what we ought to have done!"

Whoever wishes to be great among you must be your servant, and whoever wishes to be first among you must be your slave; just as the Son of Man came not to be served but to serve, and to give his life as a ransom for many.

1. Mt 18:3–4. 2. Lk 18:10–14. 3. Lk 17:7–10. 4. Mt 20:26–28. (NRSV)

*

Reading Nine

Before the festival of the Passover, Jesus, knowing that his hour had come to pass from this world to the Father, having loved those who were his in the world, loved them to the end.

They were at supper, and the devil had already put it into the mind of Judas Iscariot son of Simon, to betray him. Jesus knew that the Father had put everything into his hands, and that he had come from God and was returning to God, and he got up from table, removed his outer garments and, taking a towel, wrapped it round his waist; he then poured water into a basin and began to wash the disciples' feet and to wipe them with the towel he was wearing.

When he had washed their feet and put on his outer garments again he went back to the table. "Do you understand", he said, "what I have done to you? You call me Master and Lord, and rightly; so I am. If I, then, the Lord and Master, have washed your feet, you must wash each other's feet. I have given you an example so that you may copy what I have done to you.

"In all truth I tell you, no servant is greater than his master, no messenger is greater than the one who sent him.

"Now that you know this, blessed are you if you behave accordingly."

An argument also began between them about who should be reckoned the greatest; but he said to them,

"Among the gentiles it is the kings who lord it over them, and those who have authority over them are given the title Benefactor. With you this must not happen. No; the greatest among you must behave as if he were the youngest, the leader as if he were the one who serves. For who is the greater: the one at table or the one who serves? The one at table, surely? Yet here am I among you as one who serves!"

"This is my commandment: love one another, as I have loved you. No one can have greater love than to lay down his life for his friends."

1. Jn 13:1–5. 2. Jn 13:12–17. 3. Lk 22:24–27. 4. Jn 15:12–13. (NJB)

SECTION

II

SELF

SELF

Part 1

In Reading Ten we will again hear Jesus say, "This is my commandment: love one another as I love you. No one has greater love than this, to lay down one's life for one's friends." A suitable interpretation of the phrase "to lay down one's life" is "to put aside the manner in which one could be living." To love greatly you must sometimes let go of what you want for yourself so that someone else might be better off. You have certainly done this, haven't you? For example, haven't you ever interrupted a pleasant activity in order to help a person in trouble? Haven't you ever decided against spending money on expensive clothing for the good of the family budget? Haven't you ever let a mother and her little baby take your cosy seat on the bus? How many of these kinds of things have you done in the past year alone, or the past week? Pause for a moment and think about it. That is how you should love. Keep on this path. Be prepared to lay down your life in other ways for people you know as well as for strangers.

This is not to say that we are to deny ourselves a reasonable degree of physical and mental well-being. We have to fulfil some of our legitimate aspirations; we need a moderate amount of recreation and socializing; it is right to reserve time for seeing and appreciating God's marvellous universe.

The readings of this chapter concentrate on three areas. The first is ourselves. Jesus says, "Whoever loves his life loses it, and whoever hates his life in this world will preserve it for eternal life." "To hate" is from a Semitic term which means "to love less" or "to prefer less." If we love less our life-in-this-world we will keep it safe for life-eternal, that is, participation in the life of God. It is in not clutching mindlessly to our mortal life that God's life begins to come into our hearts.

This means, for instance, that we should stop chasing after every temporal pleasure, but leave space to carry out our spiritual responsibilities; it means that we should not manipulate always to our own advantage and convenience; it means that we should hold in check the desire to implement invariably all our ideas and plans.

It also means that we must renounce sin.

To avoid sin, it is important to pray. To avoid sin, it is important to stay away from occasions and places which are sources of temptation.

Jesus says, "You have heard that it was said, 'You shall not commit adultery.' But I say to you, everyone who looks at a woman with lust has already committed adultery with her in his heart" (Mt 5:27–28 NAB).

"Things that cause sin will inevitably occur, but woe to the person through whom they occur. It would be better

for him if a millstone were put around his neck and he be thrown into the sea than for him to cause one of these little ones to sin" (Lk 17:1–2, NAB).

"For if anyone in this sinful and adulterous generation is ashamed of me and of my words, the Son of man will also be ashamed of him when he comes in the glory of his Father with the holy angles" (Mk 8:38, NJB).

The second area is money. In the eleventh reading, Jesus says, "No one can serve two masters; for either he will hate the first and love the second, or he will be devoted to the first and despise the second. You cannot serve God and Money."

"Anyone who is trustworthy in little things is trustworthy in great; anyone who is dishonest in little things is dishonest in great. If then you are not trustworthy with money, that tainted thing, who will trust you with genuine riches" (Lk 16:10–11, NJB)? If Jesus can trust that we will consider money as something for use and not a substance to hoard, as a servant and not a precious object that can be allowed to take our love away from God and neighbour, then he will lead us to real treasures. If he can trust that we will not defend our materialistic behaviour with rationalizations such as the following – "I must be well-supplied for my retirement and for the ample comfort of my family, therefore I cannot give to the poor; besides, my funds are tied up in investments, all my spare cash has to generate interest just to keep up with inflation; I am busy every day trying to increase revenue for my company and shareholders, therefore I cannot waste any energy on unprofitable holy exercises and sentiments; my friends and relatives have

exorbitant incomes, so at all costs I must cling full-time to my distinguished and handsomely paid career in order that no one can look down on me" – then he will show us what is truly valuable.

Be careful! People who submerge themselves in the deceptive brightness of money may be ruled by darkness. We do well to ponder whether we, too, are unsuspecting slaves of this beguiling ruler. In addition to the above examples, we might also recall arguments with our spouse or children. How many of these came about because of the exaggerated importance we placed on money? We might recall the months we spent in dejection and regret for failing to profit from a business opportunity, or missed squeezing every penny out of a commercial transaction. Remember how we fretted when someone cheated a few coins off us? Remember how we walked shamefully away from the less fortunate, even though we could well have afforded to give?

The third area is a person's relationship with God and his priorities. In Reading Twelve, Jesus presents this parable: "There was a rich man whose land yielded a good harvest. He debated with himself: 'What am I to do? I have not the space to store my produce. This is what I will do,' said he: 'I will pull down my barns and build them bigger. I will collect in them all my grain and other goods, and I will say to myself, "You have plenty of good things laid by, enough for many years to come: take life easy, eat, drink, and enjoy yourself."' But God said to him, 'You fool, this very night you must surrender your life; and the money you have made, who will get it now?' That is how it is with the man who piles

up treasure for himself and remains *a pauper in the sight of God.*"

Do not get this wrong. Jesus is not against enjoyment of the fruits of one's labours. The fault of the man in the parable is not in his wealth, but in his poverty towards what matters to the Lord. There are saintly well-off people, like Abraham of old, but there are also those, rich and poor alike, who leave God out of their consciousness. They treat him as an irrelevant nobody. They pay little heed to his ways. They have scant regard for Jesus or for the ones with whom he identifies himself – the destitute, the suffering, the vulnerable, the powerless.

Listen to what they will hear at the Last Judgement if they persist in their indifference. "A curse is on you; go from my sight to the eternal fire that is ready for the devil and his angels. For when I was hungry, you gave me nothing to eat; when thirsty, nothing to drink; when I was a stranger, you did not welcome me; when I was naked, you did not clothe me; when I was ill and in prison, you did not come to my help… Truly I tell you: anything you failed to do for one of these, however insignificant, you failed to do for me."

How will such persons have a chance of entering the kingdom of heaven? Indeed, what can individuals who suppose they are sufficient unto themselves do in order to be saved? Is there any possibility of eternal life for those who routinely shun their Creator? "By human resources it is impossible, but not for God: because for God everything is possible" (Mk 10:27, NJB). In other words, they must return the Lord to the place of primacy

in their lives! "Set your mind on God's kingdom and his justice *before everything else*, and all the rest will come to you as well."

Jesus says, "Do not store up for yourselves treasure on earth, where moth and rust destroy, and thieves break in and steal; but store up treasure in heaven" (Mt 6:19–20, REB). He promised: "Amen, I say to you, there is no one who has given up house or brothers or sisters or mother or father or children or lands for my sake and for the sake of the gospel who will not receive a hundred times more now in this present age: houses and brothers and sisters and mothers and children and lands, with persecutions, and eternal life in the age to come. But many that are first will be last, and the last will be first" (Mk 10:29–31, NAB). Jesus is telling us to put him and the gospel ahead of earthly attachments. If the buying and selling of lands and houses cut into our prayer time and Sunday worship, we must resist. If, in endeavouring to please a relative, we are tempted to violate our faith, we must not give in. If the effort to satisfy our craving for luxury diverts us from God, we must change. Our loyalty to Jesus will not go unrewarded.

The finest investment we can make for ourselves is in heavenly treasure. It is the best inheritance we can leave to those dearest in our hearts. It is the loftiest gift we can bestow on our fellow human beings, especially the weak. And the way to build up treasure in heaven is by a life of reverence and love towards God and his creatures, expressed in part through alms-giving. "Sell your possessions and give to charity."

It should be made very clear that God is not interested in our money, but our hearts. It is not how much of our surplus abundance we give that he wants, but how much of ourselves. This is borne out emphatically in Jesus' praise of the lady in the following incident. "As Jesus looked up and saw rich people dropping their gifts into the chest of the temple treasury, he noticed a poor widow putting in two tiny coins. 'I tell you this,' he said: 'this poor widow has given more than any of them; for those others who have given had more than enough, but she, with less than enough, has given all she had to live on'" (Lk 21:1–4, REB).

In Reading Thirteen, he reminds us: "You shall love the Lord your God with all your heart, and with all your soul, and with all your mind." It is not prosperity or a life of glamour and endless entertainment that we should love. It is God, first and foremost. "If you love me, you will keep my commandments. And I will ask the Father, and he will give you another Advocate, to be with you forever. This is the Spirit of truth, whom the world cannot receive, because it neither sees him nor knows him. You know him, because he abides with you and he will be in you." The Holy Spirit is someone that the worldly ignore. They are so mesmerized by the delights of material things that they have no room for him. They are so blinded by their obsession to be "in," to parade their familiarity with the latest fads, to scoop everybody with the most recent rumours, to buy the newest toys on the market, to eat at the trendiest restaurants, that they do not notice his presence and guidance. But they will – as soon as they turn to God in love, and obey what he says.

"If you continue in my word, you are truly my disciples; and you will know the truth, and the truth will make you free." This is a recurring theme: when we persevere in keeping Jesus' commandments, instead of being restricted, we are genuinely liberated. As we love him, as we love our neighbour, we become less and less self-centred; while that is happening, we begin to gain insights into what life really is. We begin to discern what is good for us and what isn't. We begin to differentiate between what brings lasting happiness and what doesn't. We begin to comprehend what is necessary and what is of no consequence. We begin to know the truth. And the truth sets us free. It frees us from the oppression of pagan anxieties. It frees us to discover God's protection and care. It frees us to experience his joy and peace.

The Beatitudes are introduced in Reading Fourteen. "Blessed are those whose hearts are pure; they shall see God." The pure of heart are those whose intentions and dispositions are not mixed or insincere, but clean and straightforward. They do not say one thing and do another. They do not profess faith in Jesus and act as if he does not exist. They do not take his commandments and twist their meaning to fit their behaviour. They do not utter with their lips, "Your kingdom come, your will be done," but desire inwardly, "My kingdom come, my will be done." The pure of heart will "see God." They will recognize the Holy Spirit. They will perceive his plans at every turn. They will look for his counsel, and find it.

"Blessed are the poor in spirit; the kingdom of Heaven is theirs." This is the first Beatitude. The poor in spirit in

the Gospel according to Matthew are those who know their need of God. They understand that God is the one who upholds them, that it is he who provides for them. Hence, they do not display the arrogance or ugly assertiveness of some who are rich. Neither do they pretend to be what they are not, nor look for ways to boast. Their inability to match others does not fill them with depression or contempt. Their reliance is not on their own importance, but on God. How blessed they are. "The kingdom of Heaven is theirs." God's life is in them, right now!

Sometimes it is consoling to read a Beatitude without its second part. Concentrate on the first line. "Blessed are the sorrowful." It is in the present tense. How blessed you are, starting this minute, when you choose to follow Jesus, knowing full well that you may have to endure hardships and tribulation. How blessed you are when, in turning your back on the inordinate accumulation of wealth, you do not have all the comforts that others have. They possess beautiful houses and cars, they wear glittering jewellery and up-to-date fashions, they attend lavish parties and enjoy fabulous food and holidays, whereas you encounter deprivation and derision on your journey with Jesus. How blessed you are.

One meaning of "blessed" is "happy." Jesus is saying, "Happy are the sorrowful." A disciple's reaction to shortages, difficulties, pain or sickness, is not sadness or fear. He knows that, because of his particular set of problems, God pays special attention to him. God's favour rests upon him. So he does not go around explaining himself to everybody and soliciting pity. He

does not take every opportunity to moan and groan:
"Life is so boring sometimes. I have so many hidden
headaches. I am such a martyr but no one appreciates it.
I have done much yet few people are grateful for more
than a few days."

Jesus' disciple is not a person of whining and
complaining. He is full of joy and hope. He rejoices
under the most trying circumstances. When things go
well, he remains humble, knowing that tomorrow may
not run as smoothly. On days of desolation, he does not
despair, remembering that better times always come
again. He has to deal frequently with evil, yet he never
ceases to trust God in every situation. He is at peace. He
finds consolation in the Lord's silent companionship.
His cheerfulness brightens the lives of all who meet him.

"Blessed are those who hunger and thirst to see right
prevail." One often-missed interpretation of this
Beatitude is: blessed are those who have become hungry
and thirsty so that what is right should be done. In
response to Jesus' teaching they are spending less on
eating and drinking and committing more of their
savings to the service of the Lord and of the poor; their
willingness to put aside the manner in which they could
be living makes them happy to cut down on good food,
and to stay away from expensive places and things. How
blessed they are. It is to them that Jesus will say, "Come,
you who are blessed by my Father. Inherit the kingdom
prepared for you from the foundation of the world. For I
was hungry and you gave me food, I was thirsty and you
gave me drink" (Mt 25:34–35, NAB).

How blessed you are if, at least once in a while, individually or through an institution, you do this: "But when you give a banquet, invite the poor, the crippled, the lame, and the blind. And you will be blessed, because they cannot repay you, for you will be repaid at the resurrection of the righteous" (Lk 14:13–14, NRSV).

How blessed you are if you seek to serve instead of worrying about having fun or making money every instant of your existence. How blessed you are if you lay down your life for the love of God and neighbour. How blessed you are if you decide to change instead of hanging on to the conventions of the world.

How blessed you are if, in order to do what is virtuous and just, you go against prevalently accepted dishonest practices and other forms of misconduct. How blessed you are if ridicule and loneliness do not deter you from following the Lord's commands. How blessed you are if your master is Jesus and not popularity or social status.

How blessed you are if you spend some time in prayer instead of wasting away all day long in front of the television set and the radio. How blessed you are! How blessed you are!

Prayer

God, sometimes, because of my pursuits and interests, I do not stop to care for people who need me.

Sometimes, because of my worries and fears, I forget your commands and promises.

Often enough, I leave you at the bottom of my list of priorities, and I even neglect to pray.

Jesus, help me not to be engrossed in myself.

Your way will disrupt my plans, but then your power will be at work.

If only I would let go!

There will be trials, but I must not be afraid; instead, I must learn to listen to you.

Your light and peace are not far from those who hear.

Again meditate on Jesus' words now. Linger over all these readings. It is good to review them periodically.

Reading Ten

This is my commandment: love one another as I love you. No one has greater love than this, to lay down one's life for one's friends.

Amen, amen, I say to you, unless a grain of wheat falls to the ground and dies, it remains just a grain of wheat; but if it dies, it produces much fruit. Whoever loves his life loses it, and whoever hates his life in this world will preserve it for eternal life.

If you wish to enter into life, keep the commandments... 'You shall not kill; you shall not commit adultery; you shall not steal; you shall not bear false witness; honor your father and your mother'; and 'you shall love your neighbor as yourself.'

1. Jn 15:12–13.   2. Jn 12:24–25.   3. Mt 19:17,18–19. (NAB)

*

Reading Eleven

Beware! Be on your guard against greed of every kind, for even when someone has more than enough, his possessions do not give him life.

The lamp of the body is the eye. If your eyes are sound, you will have light for your whole body; if your eyes are bad, your whole body will be in darkness. If then the only light you have is darkness, how great a darkness that will be.

No one can serve two masters; for either he will hate the first and love the second, or he will be devoted to the first and despise the second. You cannot serve God and Money.

1. Lk 12:15. 2. Mt 6:22–24. (REB)

*

Reading Twelve

There was a rich man whose land yielded a good harvest. He debated with himself: "What am I to do? I have not the space to store my produce. This is what I will do," said he: "I will pull down my barns and build them bigger. I will collect in them all my grain and other goods, and I will say to myself, 'You have plenty of good things laid by, enough for many years to come: take life easy, eat, drink, and enjoy yourself.'" But God said to him, "You fool, this very night you must surrender your life; and the money you have made, who will get it now?" That is how it is with the man who piles up treasure for himself and remains a pauper in the sight of God.

When the Son of Man comes in his glory and all the angels with him, he will sit on his glorious throne, with all the nations gathered before him. He will separate people into two groups, as a shepherd separates the sheep from the goats; he will place the sheep on his right hand and the goats on his left... Then he will say to those on his left, "A curse is on you; go from my sight to the eternal fire that is ready for the devil and his angels. For when I was hungry, you gave me nothing to eat; when thirsty, nothing to drink; when I was a stranger, you did not welcome me; when I was naked, you did not clothe me; when I was ill and in prison, you did not come to my help." And they in their turn will reply, "Lord, when was it that we saw you hungry or thirsty or a stranger or naked or ill or in prison, and did nothing for you?" And he will answer, "Truly I tell you: anything you failed to do for one of these, however insignificant, you failed to do for me." And they will go away to eternal punishment.

Sell your possessions and give to charity. Provide for yourselves purses that do not wear out, and never-failing treasure in heaven, where no thief can get near it, no moth destroy it. For where your treasure is, there will your heart be also.

Set your mind on God's kingdom and his justice before everything else, and all the rest will come to you as well.

1. Lk 12:16–21. 2. Mt 25:31–33, 41–46. 3. Lk 12:33–34. 4. Mt 6:33. (REB)

Reading Thirteen

"You shall love the Lord your God with all your heart, and with all your soul, and with all your mind." This is the greatest and first commandment. And a second is like it: "You shall love your neighbor as yourself."

If you love me, you will keep my commandments. And I will ask the Father, and he will give you another Advocate, to be with you forever. This is the Spirit of truth, whom the world cannot receive, because it neither sees him nor knows him. You know him, because he abides with you, and he will be in you.

If you continue in my word, you are truly my disciples; and you will know the truth, and the truth will make you free.

1. Mt 22:37–39. 2. Jn 14:15–17. 3. Jn 8:31–32. (NRSV)

*

Reading Fourteen

Blessed are the poor in spirit; the kingdom of Heaven is theirs.
Blessed are the sorrowful; they shall find consolation.
Blessed are the gentle; they shall have the earth for their possession.

Blessed are those who hunger and thirst to see right prevail; they shall be satisfied.

Blessed are those who show mercy; mercy shall be shown to them.

Blessed are those whose hearts are pure; they shall see God.

Blessed are the peacemakers; they shall be called God's children.

Blessed are those who are persecuted in the cause of right; the kingdom of Heaven is theirs.

Blessed are you, when you suffer insults and persecution and calumnies of every kind for my sake. Exult and be glad, for you have a rich reward in heaven; in the same way they persecuted the prophets before you.

But alas for you who are rich; you have had your time of happiness.

Alas for you who are well fed now; you will go hungry.

Alas for you who laugh now; you will mourn and weep.

Alas for you when all speak well of you; that is how their fathers treated the false prophets.

There was once a rich man, who used to dress in purple and the finest linen, and feasted sumptuously every day. At his gate lay a poor man named Lazarus, who was covered with sores. He would have been glad to satisfy his hunger with the scraps from the rich man's table. Dogs used to come and lick his sores. One day the poor man died and was carried away by the angels to be with Abraham. The rich man also died and was buried. In Hades, where he was in torment, he looked up and there,

far away, was Abraham with Lazarus close beside him. "Abraham, my father," he called out, "take pity on me! Send Lazarus to dip the tip of his finger in water, to cool my tongue, for I am in agony in this fire." But Abraham said, "My child, remember that the good things fell to you in your lifetime, and the bad to Lazarus. Now he has his consolation here and it is you who are in agony. But that is not all: there is a great gulf fixed between us; no one can cross it from our side to reach you, and none may pass from your side to us." "Then, father," he replied, "will you send him to my father's house, where I have five brothers, to warn them, so that they may not come to this place of torment?" But Abraham said, "They have Moses and the prophets; let them listen to them." "No, father Abraham," he replied, "but if someone from the dead visits them, they will repent." Abraham answered, "If they do not listen to Moses and the prophets they will pay no heed even if someone should rise from the dead."

1. Mt 5:3–12. 2. Lk 6:24–26. 3. Lk 16:19–31. (REB)

SELF

Part 2

Who Is Jesus? What Sort of Man Is He?

Much faith is needed to accept and carry out the teachings of Jesus. That is why this chapter will deal primarily with faith. The word, however, has several connotations. Here, we will concentrate on faith as trust in Jesus, as confidence and belief in him.

A related topic concerns knowing Jesus. By that we do not refer to knowledge gained solely through the mind. We learn it through inspiration by the Holy Spirit and personal involvement. We need to step out courageously to grasp it first-hand. The reader is invited to participate in the discovery process by replying to the questions posed throughout this chapter.

As well, what we are doing includes the subject of asking God to answer our prayers.

And we will be looking not only at Jesus' sayings, but also at some of the miracles he performed.

This is the first one.

On that day, when evening had come, he said to them, "Let us go across to the other side." And leaving the crowd behind, they took him with them in the boat, just as he was. Other boats were with him. A great windstorm arose, and the waves beat into the boat, so that the boat was already being swamped. But he was in the stern, asleep on the cushion; and they woke him up and said to him, "Teacher, do you not care that we are perishing?" He woke up and rebuked the wind, and said to the sea, "Peace! Be still!" Then the wind ceased, and there was a dead calm. He said to them, "Why are you afraid? Have you still no faith?" And they were filled with great awe and said to one another, "Who then is this, that even the wind and the sea obey him?"

(Mk 4:35–41, NRSV)

What did the disciples do that caused Jesus to say, "Have you still no faith?" Please take part in the exercise and re-examine the passage to find out.

Have you yourself ever said to Jesus, "Teacher, do you not care that we are perishing?" Have you ever spoken to him as if he were asleep and had forgotten about you?

After the miracle, the question the men put to each other was, "Who then is this?" That is one of two main questions we invite the reader to ponder in this chapter. When I pray to Jesus, just to whom do I think I am speaking?

The question is phrased differently when the incident is reported in the Gospel according to Matthew.

The men were astonished at what had happened, and exclaimed, "What sort of man is this? Even the wind and the sea obey him."

(Mt 8:27, REB)

What sort of man is this Jesus from whom we often request favours? That is the other main question we ask the reader to contemplate.

Here is a second miracle.

And early in the morning he came walking toward them on the sea. But when the disciples saw him walking on the sea, they were terrified, saying, "It is a ghost!" And they cried out in fear. But immediately Jesus spoke to them and said, "Take heart, it is I; do not be afraid."

Peter answered him, "Lord, if it is you, command me to come to you on the water." He said, "Come." So Peter got out of the boat, started walking on the water, and came toward Jesus. But when he noticed the strong wind, he became frightened, and beginning to sink, he cried out, "Lord, save me!" Jesus immediately reached out his hand and caught him, saying to him, "You of little faith, why did you doubt?"

(Mt 14:25–31, NRSV)

What was Peter's problem? What caused it?

The next miracle reveals not a lack of faith but an abundance of it.

And as Jesus passed on from there, two blind men followed him, crying out, "Son of David, have pity on us!" When he entered the house, the blind men approached him and Jesus said to them, "Do you believe that I can do this?" "Yes, Lord," they said to him. Then he touched their eyes and said, "Let it be done for you according to your faith." And their eyes were opened.

(Mt 9:27–30, NAB)

How greatly Jesus regards faith! "Let it be done for you *according to your faith*." The two blind men could not even see Jesus; they simply believed in him. And because of their belief, their sight was restored.

This tremendous faith in Jesus can be yours, too. To help it grow, we recommend that you follow to the letter two specific commands of Jesus. The first one is:

In praying, do not babble like the pagans, who think that they will be heard because of their many words. Do not be like them. Your Father knows what you need before you ask him.

(Mt 6:7–8, NAB)

This is the prayer of petition. When you ask God for anything, ask very briefly. If you use many words, Jesus says you are behaving like pagans. You know what pagans are – they have no faith in God. Moreover, when you rattle on and on, you are often instructing God. But God requires no instructions. He knows your needs even before you open your mouth.

Few words are employed by the supplicants in the above story, and in the following ones.

> After he had come down from the mountain large crowds followed him. Suddenly a man with a virulent skin-disease came up and bowed low in front of him saying, "Lord, if you are willing, you can cleanse me." Jesus stretched out his hand and touched him saying, "I am willing. Be cleansed." And his skin-disease was cleansed at once.
>
> (Mt 8:1–3, NJB)

What was the leper's prayer?
Find the prayer of the next person.

> Then suddenly a woman who had been suffering from hemorrhages for twelve years came up behind him and touched the fringe of his cloak, for she said to herself, "If I only touch his cloak, I will be made well." Jesus turned, and seeing her he said, "Take heart, daughter; your faith has made you well." And instantly the woman was made well.
>
> (Mt 9:20–22, NRSV)

What was her prayer? Did she say anything to Jesus? Did she make a big fuss? Did she hang onto as much of Jesus' cloak as she could, or did she merely make contact with a tiny corner of it? Jesus was so impressed that he healed her immediately.

The second recommendation for us to grow stronger in faith is this: don't worry.

Jesus said,

> Can any of you by worrying add a single moment to your life-span? ... Learn from the way the wild flowers grow. They do not work or spin. But I tell you that not even Solomon in all his splendor was clothed like one of them. If God so clothes the grass of the field, which grows today and is thrown into the oven tomorrow, will he not much more provide for you, O you of little faith? So do not worry.
>
> (Mt 6:27, 28–31, NAB)

Would you like to stop and pinpoint your worries? Some of mine are revealed in these thoughts: "Is Jesus willing to give me what I ask? Does he care? I have not been perfectly good lately – my guilty feelings and troubled conscience probably mean he will not listen to me. It is very easy to lose favour with God. What I am asking is so impossible, I doubt if he has the power to work this miracle. Does he even do this sort of thing? How is he going to help? Will his help come in time? Will he make me wait interminably? Will I be put to shame? Will he give me exactly what I want, or will he substitute something I do not like? If he does make a substitution, will it satisfy me? And even if my wish is fulfilled, will it be a permanent reality or only a temporary illusion?"

What are your anxieties?

Here is the next miracle.

> When he looked up and saw a large crowd coming toward him, Jesus said to Philip, "Where are we to buy bread for these people to eat?" He said this to test him, for he himself knew what he was going to do. Philip answered him, "Six months' wages would not buy enough bread for each of them to get a little." One of his disciples, Andrew, Simon Peter's brother, said to him, "There is a boy here who has five barley loaves and two fish. But what are they among so many people?" Jesus said, "Make the people sit down." Now there was a great deal of grass in the place; so they sat down, about five thousand in all. Then Jesus took the loaves, and when he had given thanks, he distributed them to those who were seated; so also the fish, as much as they wanted.
>
> (Jn 6:5–11, NRSV)

What did Jesus do? He made the people sit! It was after they had sat down that he passed out the food. When we ask Jesus for something, let us, too, be spiritually seated. Let our fears subside. Let our apprehensiveness come to rest. Let peace descend on our emotions. Let Jesus dispense his gifts to us who remain calm and disciplined.

When the miracle was reported in the Gospel according to Mark, this sentence was added: "They all ate and were satisfied" (Mk 6:42, NAB). What was dry bread and stale fish, touched by Jesus' hand, became delicious and satisfying. Jesus satisfies. He satisfies all.

Do not be anxious. Jesus did not say, "Ask, and perhaps, if you deserve it, you might receive. Search, and sometimes, if you are lucky, you might find. Knock, and if I feel like it, I might open the door." No. He said:

> Ask, and it will be given to you; search, and you will find; knock, and the door will be opened to you. Everyone who asks receives; everyone who searches finds; everyone who knocks will have the door opened. Is there anyone among you who would hand his son a stone when he asked for bread? Or would hand him a snake when he asked for a fish? If you, then, evil as you are, know how to give your children what is good, how much more will your Father in heaven give good things to those who ask him?
>
> (Mt 7:7–11, NJB)

When God gives, it is never anything that can harm you. If what you ask is harmful, he will not grant that version of your request. His substitution will satisfy the deepest longings of your heart, ones you may not even be conscious of. He will give at the right time and at the right place, for he knows how to provide for his children.

Please, then, when you ask God for anything, use very few words; and after asking, do not worry. Your Father will not fail you.

The following passages describe several of Jesus' followers whose faith was severely tested. One betrayed him. One denied him. All deserted him.

And suddenly while he was still speaking, Judas, one of the Twelve, appeared, and with him a large number of men armed with swords and clubs, sent by the chief priests and elders of the people. Now the traitor had arranged a sign with them saying, "The one I kiss, he is the man. Arrest him."

(Mt 26:47–48, NJB)

Then the disciples all deserted him and fled.

(Mt 26:56, NRSV)

Then they arrested him and led him away. They brought him to the high priest's house, and Peter followed at a distance. They lit a fire in the middle of the courtyard and sat round it, and Peter sat among them. A serving-maid who saw him sitting in the firelight stared at him and said, "This man was with him too." But he denied it: "I do not know him," he said.

(Lk 22:54–57, REB)

Try to answer these questions: Why did Judas betray Jesus? Did he not like the kind of kingdom Jesus wanted to establish? Did he lose faith in Jesus' vision of life? Why did the apostles desert him? Were they fearful for their personal safety? Did they lose faith in Jesus' way? Why did Peter deny Jesus? Was he ashamed of him? Did he lose faith in his Master?

Notice that when Peter said, "I do not know him," his intention was deceit. He meant to lie, but in fact, and unwittingly, he told the truth. He certainly did not know

Jesus. At Caesarea Philippi, Jesus had asked, "But who do you say I am?" Peter had answered, "You are the Messiah, the Son of the living God" (Mt 16:16, NRSV). But what did that really mean to Peter? How did that answer affect his actions? Was he any better for saying it?

What happens when you pray the Creed, "I believe in God"? Does it influence your decisions? Does it improve your conduct? Does it allay your fears in times of crisis?

The Chinese term for crisis is *wei-ji*. By itself, the word *wei* means "dangers," and *ji* alone means "opportunities." When we go through a crisis, we often see the dangers, but seldom do we notice the opportunities. We pray to Jesus, begging him for protection, imploring him to remove obstacles and to get us out of the storm. Often, it seems that Jesus does not hear. His answer is so slow in coming that we begin to panic. We doubt if the menace will ever pass away. But do we ever wonder why Jesus delays? Can it be that he wants us to look at the opportunities – the opportunities to change, to grow, to do things differently? Can it be that he wants us to use this interruption to view our troubles from another angle, to have a deeper understanding of our human condition, of our limitations and the limitations placed on all mortal beings by time, space, and the nature of creation? Can it be that he wants us to pay closer attention to someone who needs us, or to refine our bonding with those who are near?

Perhaps he wants us to dwell on a state of affairs that requires correction. Perhaps he wants us to terminate an

illicit relationship. Perhaps he wants us to avoid taking part in a certain activity, or to discard a bad habit.

Maybe he is awaiting our consent to a job he wants us to perform. Maybe he is asking us to include him as a partner in the projects we undertake. Maybe he wants us to spend more time with him in prayer. Maybe he wants us to trust him in complete surrender.

If your faith is weak now, do not be disheartened. Learn from the apostles. As you can see, they were no better than most people: their belief in Jesus collapsed pitifully on the night of Holy Thursday. They were stunned. They were shattered. Their dreams fell apart. Yet barely three days after that terrifying evening of betrayal, desertion and denial, and after Jesus subsequently suffered, died and rose again, they began to learn the true meaning of faith. Three days! A very short time.

Watch what happened on the third apparition of Jesus after his resurrection. (This is the last miracle presented in the chapter.)

> After these things Jesus showed himself again to the disciples by the Sea of Tiberias; and he showed himself in this way. Gathered there together were Simon Peter, Thomas called the Twin, Nathanael of Cana in Galilee, the sons of Zebedee, and two others of his disciples. Simon Peter said to them, "I am going fishing." They said to him, "We will go with you." They went out and got into the boat, but that night they caught nothing.

Just after daybreak, Jesus stood on the beach; but the disciples did not know that it was Jesus. Jesus said to them, "Children, you have no fish, have you?" They answered him, "No." He said to them, "Cast the net to the right side of the boat, and you will find some." So they cast it, and now they were not able to haul it in because there were so many fish. That disciple whom Jesus loved said to Peter, "It is the Lord!" When Simon Peter heard that it was the Lord, he put on some clothes, for he was naked, and jumped into the sea. But the other disciples came in the boat, dragging the net full of fish, for they were not far from the land, only about a hundred yards off.

When they had gone ashore, they saw a charcoal fire there, with fish on it, and bread. Jesus said to them, "Bring some of the fish that you have just caught." So Simon Peter went aboard and hauled the net ashore, full of large fish, a hundred fifty-three of them; and though there were so many, the net was not torn. Jesus said to them, "Come and have breakfast." Now none of the disciples dared to ask him, "Who are you?" *because they knew it was the Lord.*

(Jn 21:1–12, NRSV)

Finally! They came to know Jesus. And not only did they know who he was, they understood now what he was like: the all-seeing, all-caring, and all-powerful Lord. In the serenity of the early morning, they sat down with him in silence. Few words needed to be spoken as

they ate what he served. Former anxieties had vanished. In their place came trust, and peace.

The transformation of the faith of the disciples took several years, but the crucial stage happened in a matter of days. We can hasten the arrival of that crucial stage of our own faith transformation by following these two injunctions without compromise: "In praying, do not babble like the pagans," and, "Do not worry." Obey them tenaciously, neither veering to the right nor the left. Hold fast to Jesus' word. Then watch your faith increase and soar. You will begin to discover the miracles he is working in your life. You will begin to understand what a great friend he is. You will begin to experience a oneness with him that is uncomplicated and filled with joy. You will begin to know who he is. You will begin to know what he is like. You will begin to know him.

Jesus said to us in Jn 6:47 (NJB), and then to his Father in Jn 17:3 (NJB),

> In all truth I tell you, everyone who believes has eternal life.
> And eternal life is this: to know you, the only true God, and Jesus Christ whom you have sent.

If you follow the logic of these two statements, you will see that to believe is to know God, to believe is to know Jesus Christ, our Lord.

The highest praise you can extend to your loving Saviour is unqualified faith in him. Give him that praise, now and forever. Amen.

Prayer

I believe in God, the Father Almighty,
Creator of heaven and earth,
Creator of me and my loved ones,
Creator who cherishes the work of his hands.

I believe in Jesus Christ his only Son, our Lord,
who delivered himself up
so as to save us from every evil,
so that our sins may be forgiven,
so that we may know joy.

I believe in the Holy Spirit,
the Lord and giver of life,
the Lord and giver of love,
the Lord and giver of courage and wisdom.

I believe God made us as friends, not strangers.
He made us as family, not outsiders.
He made us for good, not disaster.
From this day I go forward in confidence,
in faith,
in understanding,
in peace.

SELF

Part 3

In Reading Fourteen we heard Jesus say, "Blessed are you, when you suffer insults and persecution and calumnies of every kind for my sake. Exult and be glad, for you have a rich reward in heaven; in the same way they persecuted the prophets before you." When people insult and persecute you on account of Jesus, when they tell lies about you and speak all kinds of evil against you, do not be afraid. Be glad. Be happy. Jump for joy. You are in the company of the prophets. You are in the company of the greatest prophet of all – Jesus himself.

In Reading Fifteen you will hear him say, "Remember the word I spoke to you, 'No slave is greater than his master.' If they persecuted me, they will also persecute you." You are walking in your Master's footsteps. You are becoming like him. You are what he wants you to be. "No disciple is superior to the teacher; but when fully trained, every disciple will be like his teacher" (Lk 6:40, NAB).

"You will be led before governors and kings for my sake, as a witness before them and the pagans." Governors and kings in your situation today may mean the directors of your corporation, or your immediate superior, or even your spouse. You may have to answer to them for your Christian decisions and actions. "How dare you oppose company policy with ethical concerns? Why were you not as ruthless as you could have been to this debtor? Why didn't you berate more harshly those who made mistakes? Why didn't you grab everything that was yours by right?" Do not panic when you are cross-examined. Jesus has told you beforehand that he allows you to face these people as his *witness*.

"When they hand you over, do not worry about how you are to speak or what you are to say. You will be given at that moment what you are to say. For it will not be you who speak but the Spirit of your Father speaking through you."

In Reading Sixteen Jesus says, "So do not be afraid of them. Everything now covered up will be uncovered, and everything now hidden will be made clear." Do not be distressed if people misunderstand you or accuse you unjustly. All will be revealed and set right in due course. There is no need to react rashly or defend yourself dishonourably, no call to take revenge. Keep open the lines of communication; find out the causes of friction; present your case wisely; pray for God's help. Pray for those who hurt you; they need your prayers.

At the same time, do not be envious of the apparent successes of unbelievers and wrongdoers. Sooner or later they will be exposed. God will deal with them. In the

next reading (Seventeen), Jesus says, "Just as the weeds are collected and burned up with fire, so will it be at the end of the age. The Son of Man will send his angels, and they will collect out of his kingdom all causes of sin and all evildoers, and they will throw them into the furnace of fire, where there will be weeping and gnashing of teeth. Then the righteous will shine like the sun in the kingdom of their Father."

In the same reading, the parable about the weeds among the wheat gives some insight into the problem of evil. God's enemies try constantly to destroy his people; the Lord is fully aware of this, but has perfect control of the situation. He allows the children of light to live alongside the children of darkness, absolutely confident of his transcendent and inscrutable plans. In praying for the apostles at the Last Supper, Jesus said to his Father, "I am not asking you to take them out of the world, but I ask you to protect them from the evil one" (Jn 17:15, NRSV). The disciples did not have to be removed to a sanitized environment. They could function admirably on earth, and achieve holiness, under God's protection.

In such circumstances, no doubt, there will be hardship and suffering; but if we trust God's designs and purposes, if we love him, if we lend support to one another in our difficulties, then all things will work together for good. Keep in mind Jesus' assurance: "In the world you will have trouble, but take courage, I have conquered the world" (Jn 16:33, NAB).

This does not mean that we can be any less vigilant against the forces of evil. No! It does mean, however, that we need not be afraid.

When problems come, do not mope around all day restating them again and again. Instead, begin learning from them. Start searching for good solutions. Pray for guidance. It is best to pray before seeking advice from people or from books offered at the parish library.

We turn in Reading Eighteen to a matter that can be a source of nagging scruples to Christians, namely, our lack of progress in converting some sinners. Jesus says, "If your brother does wrong, go and take the matter up with him, strictly between yourselves. If he listens to you, you have won your brother over." Be sure to attempt this. Go to the next step only if the first one fails. "But if he will not listen, take one or two others with you, so that every case may be settled on the evidence of two or three witnesses." If that does not have the desired effect, then make the third recommended move. "If he refuses to listen to them, report the matter to the congregation." If nothing comes out of that, here is what Jesus tells you to do. "And if he will not listen even to the congregation, then treat him as you would a pagan or a tax-gatherer." You are not obliged to do anything else. Leave him prayerfully in God's hands.

Yes, we should correct – lovingly, respectfully, and not through fits of anger, sarcasm, or bullying. But we must not fret if there are no immediate visible signs of what we hope to accomplish. Jesus said, "No one can come to me unless he is drawn by the Father who sent me; and I will raise him up on the last day. It is written in the prophets: 'They will all be taught by God.'" God himself will teach them. He will draw them. He will look after them in his own way.

Sometimes Jesus may use you to bring people to him, perhaps even without your awareness of it. And he will use you more often if you let him be your leader. "*Come after me*, and I will make you fishers of people" (Mt 4:19, NJB). Come after Jesus, follow him, let him lead, and you will be able to capture souls for him.

"To what shall I compare the kingdom of God? It is like yeast that a woman took and mixed in with three measures of wheat flour until the whole batch of dough was leavened" (Lk 13:20–21, NAB). The life of God diffuses itself through his faithful followers. As you do your part, others will be influenced. Therefore, adhere to Jesus' teachings and many will be affected and transformed in the course of time.

Reading Nineteen ends Section II. Again, we have a narrative. This one concerns Jesus' passion and death. At Gethsemane, Jesus is momentarily deluged by his human emotions. We are told that horror, anguish and grief come over him. He is so reluctant to accept the impending suffering that he begs his Father, "Take this cup from me." Still, his love for the Father prevails; he is willing to obey in whatever is asked of him. In the end he says, "Yet not my will but yours." Just as he taught his disciples to love him by keeping his commands, so Jesus loves his Father by obeying all that he requests.

After this, Judas betrays Jesus with a kiss. In our own relationships, let us be wary of superficial signs of comradeship. False friends will disguise their wicked agendas through seemingly amiable gestures. And never assume that false friends are found only in non-religious circles. Judas Iscariot was an apostle! Do not be

surprised that within the Church there are betrayers of Jesus. Take care not to be deceived by them.

In this reading, we see Jesus healing the servant whose ear is cut off. Instead of retaliating, he responds with kindness.

"Jesus was taken away, and went out, carrying the cross himself, to the place called The Skull (in Hebrew, 'Golgotha'); there they crucified him, and with him two others, one on either side, with Jesus in between." Jesus is now numbered among thieves. We, too, may meet the same fate. Our loyalty to Jesus can cause the world to brand us as criminal, wasteful, foolish, impractical, old-fashioned, narrow-minded, weak. For these perceived deficiencies, we may be socially crucified by our peers. The insult and disrespect can be borne in silence only because there is unflinching faith in Jesus' teachings.

In his short life on earth, Jesus was rejected many times. When you encounter rejection, do not be sad, but rejoice that, for a while, like our Lord, you have to face the rebuffs and misconceptions of scoffers.

"And at three Jesus cried aloud, 'Eloi, Eloi, lema sabachthani?' which means 'My God, my God, why have you forsaken me?'" He does not so much as feel the presence of God. Undaunted, he resolutely affirms, "Father, into your hands I commit my spirit." Even though the road seems to be heading towards disgrace and failure, he surrenders totally to his Father.

Reading Nineteen leaves us with the question of whether we, too, as followers of Jesus, will love and trust God to the extent our Master did. Will we be true to his precepts even if it costs us everything? Do we dare

place our fidelity above reputation, above ambition, above economic security? Can we let go of our elaborate plans? Are we willing to lay down our lives for Jesus just as he did for his Father?

"When the centurion who was standing opposite him saw how he died, he said, 'This man must have been a son of God.'" The centurion is a pagan, yet even he acknowledges Jesus to be a child of God. Remember the Beatitude: "Blessed are the peacemakers, for they will be called children of God" (Mt 5:9, NAB). Remember also this teaching from the second reading: "But love your enemies, do good, and lend, expecting nothing in return. Your reward will be great, and you will be children of the Most High" (Lk 6:35, NRSV). Jesus continues to love his enemies. He does not stop doing good to those who hurt him. He makes peace between God and man. These things alone are capable of inspiring people to call him a son of God. We, too, can someday be recognized by all as God's children if, in the face of evil and opposition, we remain fearlessly faithful to his commands. If we love him with all our heart and soul, paying no heed to personal prestige or safety, if we face our persecutors with heroic fortitude, if we follow Jesus even to the point of death, believing valiantly in him and his promises, then, one day, not only Christians but pagans as well, will glorify God through us with shouts of acclamation: "In truth this man is a son of God! In truth this woman is a daughter of the Most High! In truth this disciple has become just like his Master!"

Prayer

Lord, you are a loving God,
and you always hear my prayers.
Yet, when my petitions are not answered quickly,
fear creeps in; I feel helpless, my spirit grows weary.
In these times, it is important that I do not lose hope.
For you are quietly there.
You do not forget your people;
you never abandon your own.
You hold me close.
At the favourable moment, on the acceptable day,
you will grant the desires of my heart.
Lord, you choose the time,
you decide the place.
Your will be done.
Your will be done.
For your will does not lead to misery and defeat.
It is the shortest and surest way to triumphant victory.

Reading Fifteen

If the world hates you, realize that it hated me first. If you belonged to the world, the world would love its own; but because you do not belong to the world, and I have chosen you out of the world, the world hates you. Remember the word I spoke to you, "No slave is greater than his master." If they persecuted me, they will also persecute you.

You will be led before governors and kings for my sake as a witness before them and the pagans. When they hand you over, do not worry about how you are to speak or what you are to say. You will be given at that moment what you are to say. For it will not be you who speak but the Spirit of your Father speaking through you.

You will be hated by all because of my name, but whoever endures to the end will be saved. When they persecute you in one town, flee to another. Amen, I say to you, you will not finish the towns of Israel before the Son of Man comes.

Amen, amen, I say to you, you will weep and mourn, while the world rejoices; you will grieve, but your grief will become joy. When a woman is in labor, she is in anguish because her hour has arrived; but when she has given birth to a child, she no longer remembers the pain because of her joy that a child has been born into the world. So you also are now in anguish. But I will see

you again, and your hearts will rejoice, and no one will take your joy away from you.

I have told you this so that you might have peace in me. In the world you will have trouble, but take courage, I have conquered the world.

1. Jn 15:18–20. 2. Mt 10:18–20. 3. Mt 10:22–23. 4. Jn 16:20–22. 5. Jn 16:33. (NAB)

*

Reading Sixteen

Disciple is not superior to teacher, nor slave to master. It is enough for disciple to grow to be like teacher, and slave like master. If they have called the master of the house "Beelzebul", how much more the members of his household?

So do not be afraid of them. Everything now covered up will be uncovered, and everything now hidden will be made clear. What I say to you in the dark, tell in the daylight; what you hear in whispers, proclaim from the housetops.

Do not be afraid of those who kill the body but cannot kill the soul; fear him rather who can destroy both body and soul in hell. Can you not buy two sparrows for a penny? And yet not one falls to the ground without your Father knowing. Why, every hair on your head has been counted. So there is no need to be afraid; you are worth more than many sparrows.

So if anyone declares himself for me in the presence of human beings, I will declare myself for him in the presence of my Father in heaven. But the one who disowns me in the presence of human beings, I will disown in the presence of my Father in heaven.

1. Mt 10:24–33. (NJB)

*

Reading Seventeen

The kingdom of heaven may be compared to someone who sowed good seed in his field; but while everybody was asleep, an enemy came and sowed weeds among the wheat, and then went away. So when the plants came up and bore grain, then the weeds appeared as well. And the slaves of the householder came and said to him, "Master, did you not sow good seed in your field? Where, then, did these weeds come from?" He answered, "An enemy has done this." The slaves said to him, "Then do you want us to go and gather them?" But he replied, "No; for in gathering the weeds you would uproot the wheat along with them. Let both of them grow together until the harvest; and at harvest time I will tell the reapers, Collect the weeds first and bind them in bundles to be burned, but gather the wheat into my barn."

Just as the weeds are collected and burned up with fire, so will it be at the end of the age. The Son of Man will send his angels, and they will collect out of his kingdom

all causes of sin and all evildoers, and they will throw them into the furnace of fire, where there will be weeping and gnashing of teeth. Then the righteous will shine like the sun in the kingdom of their Father. Let anyone with ears listen!

1. Mt 13:24–30. 2. Mt. 13:40–43. (NRSV)

⁜

Reading Eighteen

Do not give dogs what is holy; do not throw your pearls to the pigs: they will only trample on them, and turn and tear you to pieces.

If your brother does wrong, go and take the matter up with him, strictly between yourselves. If he listens to you, you have won your brother over. But if he will not listen, take one or two others with you, so that every case may be settled on the evidence of two or three witnesses. If he refuses to listen to them, report the matter to the congregation; and if he will not listen even to the congregation, then treat him as you would a pagan or a tax-gatherer.

At any place where they will not receive you or listen to you, shake the dust off your feet as you leave, as a solemn warning.

If they do not listen to Moses and the prophets they will pay no heed even if someone should rise from the dead.

Leave them alone; they are blind guides, and if one blind man guides another they will both fall into the ditch.

No one can come to me unless he is drawn by the Father who sent me; and I will raise him up on the last day. It is written in the prophets: "They will all be taught by God."

You did not choose me: I chose you. I appointed you to go on and bear fruit, fruit that will last; so that the Father may give you whatever you ask in my name.

Follow me, and leave the dead to bury their dead.

1. Mt 7:6. 2. Mt 18:15–17. 3. Mk 6:11. 4. Lk 16:31. 5. Mt 15:14. 6. Jn 6:44–45. 7. Jn 15:16. 8. Mt 8:22. (REB)

*

Reading Nineteen

When they reached a place called Gethsemane, he said to his disciples, "Sit here while I pray." And he took Peter and James and John with him. Horror and anguish overwhelmed him, and he said to them, "My heart is ready to break with grief; stop here, and stay awake." Then he went on a little farther, threw himself on the

ground, and prayed that if it were possible this hour might pass him by. "Abba, Father," he said, "all things are possible to you; take this cup from me. Yet not my will but yours."

While he was still speaking a crowd appeared with the man called Judas, one of the Twelve, at their head. He came up to Jesus to kiss him; but Jesus said, "Judas, would you betray the Son of Man with a kiss?"

When his followers saw what was coming, they said, "Lord, shall we use our swords?" And one of them struck at the high priest's servant, cutting off his right ear. But Jesus answered, "Stop! No more of that!" Then he touched the man's ear and healed him.

Then the disciples all deserted him and ran away.

Jesus was taken away, and went out, carrying the cross himself, to the place called The Skull (in Hebrew, "Golgotha"); there they crucified him, and with him two others, one on either side, with Jesus in between.

One of the criminals hanging there taunted him: "Are not you the Messiah? Save yourself, and us." But the other rebuked him: "Have you no fear of God? You are under the same sentence as he is. In our case it is plain justice; we are paying the price for our misdeeds. But this man has done nothing wrong." And he said, "Jesus, remember me when you come to your throne." Jesus answered, "Truly I tell you: today you will be with me in Paradise."

And at three Jesus cried aloud, "Eloi, Eloi, lema sabachthani?" which means, "My God, my God, why have you forsaken me?"

Then Jesus uttered a loud cry and said, "Father, into your hands I commit my spirit"; and with these words he died.

When the centurion who was standing opposite him saw how he died, he said, "This man must have been a son of God."

1. Mk 14:32–36. 2. Lk 22:47–51. 3. Mt 26:56. 4. Jn 19:16–18. 5. Lk 23:39–43. 6. Mk 15:34. 7. Lk 23:46. 8. Mk 15:39. (REB)

SECTION

III

LIVE JESUS' GOSPEL

LIVE JESUS' GOSPEL

Part 1

In the last reading, one passage contained this line: "Then the disciples all deserted him and ran away." Have you ever deserted Jesus? Were you ever tempted to consider him superfluous? Were you ever led to follow the so-called "politically correct" convenience of dismissing him as an outmoded custom? Have you ever rejected the teachings of his Church leaders because they appeared to have fallen short of the conclusions reached through the unbiased research, infallible deductions, and exhaustive knowledge of your friends and informants?

If you have ever run away, no matter what the cause, the important question is: will you return to him now? He bears no grudges.

When Jesus predicted Peter's denial of him, he announced, "Simon, Simon, listen! Satan has demanded to sift all of you like wheat, but I have prayed for you that your own faith may not fail; and you, when once you have turned back, strengthen your brothers" (Lk 22:31–32, NRSV). Jesus is telling you also that Satan may have tried to detach you from God, shaking your

faith and dislodging your allegiance. But the Lord respected your freedom, and allowed you to move away, certain that once you have turned back you would give strength to your brothers and sisters with understanding and humility. God can draw forth good out of potentially bad situations.

If you have left Jesus, don't be afraid to change. He is waiting for you with outstretched arms. Should you ever doubt his longing for your reversal of heart or his willingness to forgive, ponder deeply the reason why he died. Even on the cross this was how he prayed: "Father, forgive them; they do not know what they are doing" (Lk 23:34, REB). He himself pardons all your weaknesses and sins, and intercedes on your behalf.

No damage is ever irreparable if one accepts and trusts Jesus. The thief crucified beside him exemplified this in such a beautiful and touching moment. He asked to be remembered when Jesus came into his kingdom, and received this promise, "Truly I tell you: today you will be with me in Paradise" (Lk 23:43, REB).

When Jesus appeared to his disciples on the night after his resurrection, this was what took place: "On the evening of that first day of the week, when the doors were locked, where the disciples were, for fear of the Jews, Jesus came and stood in their midst and said to them, 'Peace be with you.' When he had said this, he showed them his hands and his side. The disciples rejoiced when they saw the Lord. Jesus said to them again, 'Peace be with you'" (Jn 20:19–21, NAB). Notice that Jesus did not say one word of rejection. He did not harp on the group's disloyalty. He did not belittle.

Instead, he wished them peace. He greeted them with goodwill. He put their troubled hearts at ease. That is the way he behaves towards those who have deserted him temporarily. He offers himself in friendship. And "he showed them his hands and his side." In sporting his wounds, his battle scars, he demonstrated the familiarity that a man shows his friends, not his foes. "Jesus said to them *again*, 'Peace be with you,'" emphasizing his desire for reconciliation.

He went on to say, "As the Father sent me, so am I sending you." Then he breathed on them and said, "Receive the Holy Spirit" (Jn 20:21, 22, NJB). So he still wanted to treat his disciples as his Father treated him; he still wanted to send them out; he still wanted to give them the Holy Spirit. It is the same with you even if you may have abandoned him for a little while. He still wants you to be his disciple; he still wants you to be his partner in service; he still wants to pour his Spirit upon you without reserve.

"Then he opened their minds to understand the scriptures, and he said to them, 'Thus it is written, that the Messiah is to suffer and to rise from the dead on the third day, and that *repentance* and *forgiveness* of sins is to be proclaimed in his name to all nations'" (Lk 24:45–47, NRSV). He asked his disciples to preach forgiveness. If you have deserted him, do not forget this: he forgives you. Jesus also made sure that his disciples preached repentance. Turn your heart and mind away from sin and back to God.

Now we come to Section III, "Live Jesus' Gospel." To *live* Jesus' gospel means to *carry out* what he taught and

not just hear and do nothing. To live *Jesus'* gospel means to carry out *what he taught* and not the norms of pagan society. To live Jesus' gospel means, with Christian faith, going beyond the crowd whose religion is merely abstention from fatty foods, drinking eight glasses of water a day, exercising four hours each week, taking enough vitamins and herbs, holding 'intelligent' conversations, and complying with secular etiquette; it means putting Christ at the centre of the home, of Christmas, of Easter, and not the television set, not the instruments of commerce like Santa Claus and the Easter Bunny; it means honouring the name of Jesus and not using it as a swear word; it means keeping his commands: "'You shall love the Lord your God with all your heart, with all your soul, with all your mind, and with all your strength'… 'You shall love your neighbor as yourself'" (Mk 12:30, 31, NAB).

In the first reading (Twenty) of this chapter, we are told: "It is not anyone who says to me, 'Lord, Lord,' who will enter the kingdom of Heaven, but the person who does the will of my Father in heaven. When the day comes many will say to me, 'Lord, Lord, did we not prophesy in your name, drive out demons in your name, work many miracles in your name?' Then I shall tell them to their faces: I have never known you; away from me, all evil doers!" None of the deeds Jesus mentions, if done apart from the Father's will, can ever be construed as proof of true love of God. "Evil" here in the term "evil doers" means the absence of good. Evil doers are those who take part in activities (some of which may be laudable) but merit no eternal good from them. If I

march in protest against polluters of the environment, and donate hundreds of dollars to medical research, but ignore the Father's will, I gain not a single thing by it. If I read dozens of books and am very erudite in many subjects, but leave the Creator out of my life, I am nothing. If I have the gift of fine diction but waste it daily in a bid to impress people with pretentious utterances, I am just a clashing gong. If I live with little reverence for the Lord, relegating him to the last place, I may someday hear Jesus say to me: "I have never known you; away from me, all evil doers!"

Love of God is not the same as giving eye-catching performances. Holiness and wisdom do not equal having much to say. Those who think otherwise may be able to fool some people. They can certainly fool themselves. But they cannot fool God.

Let there be no misunderstanding about this: Jesus is not opposed to learning or the pursuit of excellence or the promotion of health in body, mind and soul. He does not discourage anyone from doing good.

On the contrary, he makes it abundantly clear what it is that will cause our efforts to be truly fruitful. He said, "*Remain in me*, as I in you. As a branch cannot bear fruit all by itself, unless it remains part of the vine, neither can you unless you remain in me. I am the vine, you are the branches. Whoever remains in me, with me in him, bears fruit in plenty; for cut off from me you can do nothing."

So how do we remain in Jesus? He said, "I have loved you just as the Father has loved me. Remain in my love. If you *keep my commandments* you will remain in my

love, just as I have kept my Father's commandments and remain in his love." Keep his commandments! It is when we obey Jesus that we will become productive disciples. Jesus himself obeyed his Father up to his very last breath. The harvest he was thus able to prepare is bountiful and everlasting.

He said, "You did not choose me: *I chose* you. I appointed you to go on and bear fruit, fruit that will last" (Jn 15:16, REB). Jesus does the choosing, not the other way around. He is the one who appoints his labourers, who trains them, who gives the order to go forth when they are ready. If he sends them out, the good they accomplish will endure.

In Reading Twenty-one, he says, "Beware of the yeast of the Pharisees, that is, their hypocrisy." Remember not to apply these sayings negatively. Jesus is not accusing us of hypocrisy. He is warning us to be on guard against it. Not even a tiny bit should be allowed to creep in. Like yeast, a small amount will affect the whole.

We will dwell on this subject a little longer because hypocrisy is a very dangerous shortcoming, and can lead to gross superficiality, serious error, and embarrassing disillusionment. Jesus' admonition is: "For I tell you, unless your righteousness exceeds that of the scribes and Pharisees, you will never enter the kingdom of heaven."

Of all the faults Jesus mentions, hypocrisy is the one he comments on most often. Throughout the Gospels, hypocrites arouse his severest anger. He launches the sharpest words at them. "Woe to you, scribes and Pharisees, hypocrites! For you clean the outside of the cup and of the plate, but inside they are full of greed and

self-indulgence. You blind Pharisee! First clean the inside of the cup, so that the outside also may become clean." Stop thinking you are holy when your heart is full of judging and despising, haughtiness and animosity. Stop imagining yourself an example for everyone to follow. Quit fancying that people are looking at you. Chasten yourself before you attempt to chasten others.

"You are those who justify yourselves in the sight of others; but God knows your hearts; for what is prized by human beings is an abomination in the sight of God." For instance, just by going to church in our "Sunday best" suits does not demonstrate holiness. Knowing the prayer responses and when to sit and stand during liturgy is no indication of love of Jesus. Greeting others after a religious service with suave pleasantries is merely an attempt at making ourselves appear better than we are.

Jesus says, "Isaiah prophesied rightly about you hypocrites, as it is written, 'This people honors me with their lips, but their hearts are far from me; in vain do they worship me, teaching human precepts as doctrines.' You abandon the commandment of God and hold to human tradition."

"You search the scriptures, because you think that in them you have eternal life; and it is they that testify on my behalf. Yet you refuse to come to me to have life." When we read the Bible, do we pick out only the texts we are fond of? But when we encounter passages where Jesus tells us to do something we do not like, do we skip over them quickly? Do we exempt ourselves by declaring, "These do not apply to me; they are for beginners"?

Hypocrites have a way of seeing what they want to see and no more. They remain conveniently blind to what they disapprove. Everything they do is admirable in their own sight. Whatever conforms to their lifestyle they accept as correct. They make countless rules instantly, and all of these are interpreted to fit their "philosophy." Everyone is inferior who does not know what they know. Let an "inferior" person make a suggestion, and their blood boils over. If they do not belittle and reject in public, they do so in the darkness of their hearts. Hypocrites imagine themselves wise and knowledgeable. They are, in fact, eloquently empty and ignorant.

In the same paragraph we read, "I have come in my Father's name, and you do not accept me; if another comes in his own name, you will accept him." Sometimes we begin to doubt and downgrade Jesus' teachings when we hear an opposite message from a popular person who comes along speaking what pleases our ears, someone who, because of his position of influence and university degrees, is able to charm many self-styled intellectuals. As well, we often find it comfortable to congregate with friends who give little prominence to Jesus but love instead to seek praise for each other's theories and practices. How easy it is to stop believing in what Jesus considers important. "How can you believe when you accept glory from one another and do not seek the glory that comes from the one who alone is God?"

Hypocrites expect everybody to love and respect them. At no time do they have love or respect for anyone other than themselves and a handful who are dear to them. Of

course, when people are watching, they may condescend to give some semblance of civility towards the rest of humanity.

The worst hypocrites are the irreligious ones who summarily write off others by branding them with the stigma of shallowness but do not even notice the destructive maliciousness of their own. God's critics often think they know a lot.

Now, to be fair, it must be pointed out that the human imperfections mentioned are not necessarily evidence of hypocrisy. More often than not they are unconscious habits and have no linkage to wilful or culpable blindness. The answer to the question, "Why do you see the splinter in your brother's eye but not the plank in your own?" may legitimately be, "Because I didn't know I was doing it." Some character flaws have been singled out purely in the hope that, once people are alerted, they will amend their behaviour.

In Reading Twenty-two, Jesus says, "Everyone who listens to these words of mine and acts on them will be like a wise man who built his house on rock. The rain fell, the floods came, and the winds blew and buffeted the house. But it did not collapse; it had been set solidly on rock." Jesus does not want us to fall. And we will not if, when we hear his words, we carry them out. If we are not blown about by every wind of doctrine, if we live by "these words of mine," Jesus' words, not someone else's, our foundations are solidly built. Nothing can topple us.

"And everyone who listens to these words of mine but does not act on them will be like a fool who built his

house on sand. The rain fell, the floods came, and the winds blew and buffeted the house. And it collapsed and was completely ruined."

Also in this reading, Jesus relates the parable of a king hosting a banquet for his son's marriage. "But when the king came in to meet the guests he saw a man there not dressed in a wedding garment. He said to him, 'My friend, how is it that you came in here without a wedding garment?'" Jesus is saying: "I have invited you to my kingdom; why is it you do not wear the clothes I expect you to wear? Why do you not come the way I request? Why do you not follow my instructions?"

In the next parable Jesus warns, "But if that wicked servant says to himself, 'My master is long delayed,' and begins to beat his fellow servants, and eat and drink with drunkards, the servant's master will come on an unexpected day and at an unknown hour and will punish him severely and assign him a place with the hypocrites, where there will be wailing and grinding of teeth." Sometimes we may be tempted to think, "I am a pretty respectable citizen now. Surely I should be permitted to act impolitely towards those who work beneath me; I can use foul language to express my displeasure; I can bait my spouse into petty arguments; I can dole out my mundane observations shamelessly, and often. Surely I deserve to have any kind of entertainment I choose, to drink as much as I want, to read all the latest novels, to see any movie at the theatre or watch whatever program that is shown on television; nothing can be harmful to me. I am 'successful' but dissatisfied at home, surely I can be excused if I engage in extra-marital liaisons."

Do not be guided by such thoughts. A person with these dispositions could be cut off and sent to "a place with the hypocrites, where there will be wailing and grinding of teeth." Such a person could tell himself, "My master is long delayed," meaning, "I don't have to do as he commanded just yet," and would hear Jesus say, "The servant's master will come on an unexpected day and at an unknown hour and will punish him severely." "That servant who knew his master's will but did not make preparations nor act in accord with his will shall be beaten severely… Much will be required of the person entrusted with much."

The parable in the twenty-third reading describes a landowner who, having found no fruit from his fig tree for three years, gave orders to have it chopped off. But the gardener pleaded with him. "'Sir,' the man replied, 'leave it one more year and give me time to dig round it and manure it: it may bear fruit next year; if not, then you can cut it down.'" Jesus is saying that we still have the chance to grow up! But not for long.

Please do not get the mistaken notion that Jesus has already condemned us to the punishments described in the gospel. In point of fact, the opposite is true: what he is doing is telling us how to avoid those punishments! With God's help, it actually takes very little to redirect our lives so that our gifts and energies will not be wasted, so that we can become holy, loving, and genuinely useful for the Kingdom of God. May we avail ourselves of this time of grace which God has given. May we devote some of our abilities, money and

influence to the service of God, of the poor, of the weak, of those who do not know how to help themselves.

The more gifted we are, the more should we be patient, kind, humble, polite, merciful, gentle, helpful and loving towards everyone – everyone, not just our equals or those we wish to impress, but especially those under our financial control. Let us do it sincerely for their benefit, and not to enhance our public image.

Let us also reserve time for prayer, honouring and thanking our Maker who gave us our talents and opportunities. Let us pray for the welfare of all.

What Jesus wants is found in Reading Twenty-four: "Gird your loins and light your lamps and be like servants who await their master's return from a wedding, ready to open immediately when he comes and knocks. Blessed are those servants whom the master finds vigilant on his arrival. Amen, I say to you, he will gird himself, have them recline at table, and proceed to wait on them."

In the fourth paragraph Jesus says, "The light will be among you only a little while. Walk while you have the light, so that darkness may not overcome you." Jesus urges us to walk in the light now, to live his gospel immediately, to follow him right away. Do not tarry. Start today. It is not that he won't accept us if we procrastinate. He will always forgive and welcome us. But if we persist in ignoring him, we may end up convicting ourselves, like Judas Iscariot, by hardening our hearts and refusing to go back to him.

"While you have the light, believe in the light, so that you may become children of the light." And as children

of light we will see, we will understand, for that is what light does: it enables one to see. As children of light, we will have power to illuminate the way for others so that they, too, may see. This is the light Jesus refers to when he says, "Just so, your light must shine before others, that they may see your good deeds and glorify your heavenly Father" (Mt 5:16, NAB).

There is no contradiction between the above passage and the following one: "Be careful not to parade your uprightness in public to attract attention" (Mt 6:1, NJB). If you do things just to show off, "you will lose all reward from your Father in heaven" (Mt 6:1, NJB). But when you walk with Jesus, his light radiates from within; no amount of self-trumpeting can duplicate it. Everyone knows it is given by God, and glory will not be wrongly directed to you, but to "your heavenly Father."

"If you remain in my word, you will truly be my disciples, and you will know the truth, and the truth will set you free." If you live according to "my word," that is, Jesus' word, you really and truly deserve to be called "my" disciple, Christ's disciple – Christian. You will know the truth – you will see, you will understand. And the truth will set you free, not restrict you. It will set free those to whom you give of yourself in loving service.

Prayer

God, I will make use of my resources.
I will develop my capabilities.
I will strive for perfection in worthwhile undertakings.
But I must not cling to the things that make me hollow.
It is not how highly I am esteemed which results in righteousness, but whether your word reigns over the way I live.
You do not make me all-powerful; you do not render me trouble-free.
You want me to be your child;
much good is accomplished through those who are children.
Let all thanks and praise be directed to you, Lord,
now and forever. Amen.

Reading Twenty

It is not anyone who says to me, "Lord, Lord," who will enter the kingdom of Heaven, but the person who does the will of my Father in heaven. When the day comes many will say to me, "Lord, Lord, did we not prophesy in your name, drive out demons in your name, work many miracles in your name?" Then I shall tell them to their faces: I have never known you; away from me, all evil doers!

Remain in me, as I in you. As a branch cannot bear fruit all by itself, unless it remains part of the vine, neither can you unless you remain in me. I am the vine, you are the branches. Whoever remains in me, with me in him, bears fruit in plenty; for cut off from me you can do nothing. Anyone who does not remain in me is thrown away like a branch – and withers; these branches are collected and thrown on the fire and are burnt.

I have loved you just as the Father has loved me. Remain in my love. If you keep my commandments you will remain in my love, just as I have kept my Father's commandments and remain in his love.

1. Mt 7:21–23. 2. Jn 15:4–6. 3. Jn 15:9–10. (NJB)

*

Reading Twenty-One

Beware of the yeast of the Pharisees, that is, their hypocrisy.

They do all their deeds to be seen by others.

Woe to you, scribes and Pharisees, hypocrites! For you are like whitewashed tombs, which on the outside look beautiful, but inside they are full of the bones of the dead and of all kinds of filth. So you also on the outside look righteous to others, but inside you are full of hypocrisy and lawlessness.

Woe to you, scribes and Pharisees, hypocrites! For you clean the outside of the cup and of the plate, but inside they are full of greed and self-indulgence. You blind Pharisee! First clean the inside of the cup, so that the outside also may become clean.

Woe to you, scribes and Pharisees, hypocrites! For you cross sea and land to make a single convert, and you make the new convert twice as much a child of hell as yourselves.

You are those who justify yourselves in the sight of others; but God knows your hearts; for what is prized by human beings is an abomination in the sight of God.

Isaiah prophesied rightly about you hypocrites, as it is written,

"This people honors me with their lips,
but their hearts are far from me;
in vain do they worship me,
teaching human precepts as doctrines."
You abandon the commandment of God and hold to human tradition.

You search the scriptures because you think that in them you have eternal life; and it is they that testify on my behalf. Yet you refuse to come to me to have life. I do not accept glory from human beings. But I know that you do not have the love of God in you. I have come in my Father's name, and you do not accept me; if another comes in his own name, you will accept him. How can you believe when you accept glory from one another and do not seek the glory that comes from the one who alone is God?

For I tell you, unless your righteousness exceeds that of the scribes and Pharisees, you will never enter the kingdom of heaven.

1. Lk 12:1. 2. Mt 23:5. 3. Mt 23:27–28. 4. Mt 23:25–26. 5. Mt 23:15. 6. Lk 16:15. 7. Mk 7:6–8. 8. Jn 5:39–44. 9. Mt 5:20. (NRSV)

*

Reading Twenty-Two

Everyone who listens to these words of mine and acts on them will be like a wise man who built his house on rock. The rain fell, the floods came, and the winds blew and buffeted the house. But it did not collapse; it had been set solidly on rock. And everyone who listens to these words of mine but does not act on them will be like a fool who built his house on sand. The rain fell, the floods came, and the winds blew and buffeted the house. And it collapsed and was completely ruined.

The kingdom of heaven may be likened to a king who gave a wedding feast for his son…

But when the king came in to meet the guests he saw a man there not dressed in a wedding garment. He said to him, "My friend, how is it that you came in here without a wedding garment?" But he was reduced to silence. Then the king said to his attendants, "Bind his hands and feet, and cast him into the darkness outside, where there will be wailing and grinding of teeth." Many are invited, but few are chosen.

That servant who knew his master's will but did not make preparations nor act in accord with his will shall be beaten severely; and the servant who was ignorant of his master's will but acted in a way deserving of a severe beating shall be beaten only lightly. Much will be required of the person entrusted with much, and still more will be demanded of the person entrusted with more.

Who, then, is the faithful and prudent servant, whom the master has put in charge of his household to distribute to them their food at the proper time? Blessed is that servant whom his master on his arrival finds doing so. Amen, I say to you, he will put him in charge of all his property. But if that wicked servant says to himself, "My master is long delayed," and begins to beat his fellow servants, and eat and drink with drunkards, the servant's master will come on an unexpected day and at an unknown hour and will punish him severely and assign him a place with the hypocrites, where there will be wailing and grinding of teeth.

Salt is good, but if salt itself loses its taste, with what can its flavor be restored? It is fit neither for the soil nor for the manure pile; it is thrown out. Whoever has ears to hear ought to hear.

1. Mt 7:24–27. 2. Mt 22:2, 11–14. 3. Lk 12:47–48. 4. Mt 24:45–51. 5. Lk 14:34-35. (NAB)

*

Reading Twenty-Three

A man had a fig tree planted in his vineyard, and he came looking for fruit on it but found none. He said to his vinedresser, "For three years now I have been coming to look for fruit on this fig tree and finding none. Cut it down: why should it be taking up the ground?"

"Sir," the man replied, "leave it one more year and give me time to dig round it and manure it: it may bear fruit next year; if not, then you can cut it down."

I am the true vine, and my Father is the vinedresser. Every branch in me that bears no fruit he cuts away, and every branch that does bear fruit he prunes to make it bear even more.

1. Lk 13:6–9. 2. Jn 15:1–2. (NJB)

*

Reading Twenty-Four

Gird your loins and light your lamps and be like servants who await their master's return from a wedding, ready to open immediately when he comes and knocks. Blessed are those servants whom the master finds vigilant on his arrival. Amen, I say to you, he will gird himself, have them recline at table, and proceed to wait on them.

Come to me, all you who labor and are burdened, and I will give you rest. Take my yoke upon you and learn from me, for I am meek and humble of heart; and you will find rest for yourselves. For my yoke is easy, and my burden light.

I am the light of the world. Whoever follows me will not walk in darkness, but will have the light of life.

The light will be among you only a little while. Walk while you have the light, so that darkness may not overcome you. Whoever walks in the dark does not know where he is going. While you have the light, believe in the light, so that you may become children of the light.

If you remain in my word, you will truly be my disciples, and you will know the truth, and the truth will set you free.

1. Lk 12:35–37. 2. Mt 11:28–30. 3. Jn 8:12. 4. Jn 12:35–36. 5. Jn 8:31–32. (NAB)

LIVE JESUS' GOSPEL

Part 2

To live Jesus' gospel means to act upon what he taught and not just to theorize about it. Living his gospel also means practising what is in *Jesus'* gospel, not another person's. We may be able to learn something about God from other religions and thinkers, but if we profess to be Christians, we must be committed to Christ. God said of him, "This is my Son, my Chosen; listen to him" (Lk 9:35, REB).

When Jesus appeared on earth, wise men came seeking him. "In the time of King Herod, after Jesus was born in Bethlehem of Judea, wise men from the East came to Jerusalem, asking, 'Where is the child who has been born king of the Jews? For we have observed his star at its rising, and have come to pay him homage'" (Mt 2:1–2, NRSV). When they located him, what did they do? They stopped looking for someone else! "They set out; and there, ahead of them, went the star that they had seen at its rising, until it stopped over the place where the child was. When they saw that the star had stopped,

they were overwhelmed with joy. On entering the house, they saw the child with Mary his mother; and they knelt down and paid him homage" (Mt 2:9–11, NRSV). They prostrated themselves before him. They adored him. They were thrilled to meet him and were convinced that he was the king they had set out to find.

And when they were cautioned to go home by an alternative route, they did just that. "And having been warned in a dream not to return to Herod, they left for their own country by another road" (Mt 2:12, NRSV). They changed course. They changed direction. They changed plans. And by changing, they escaped all the pitfalls and snares of their former way.

Be like wise men. Having found Jesus, be sensible enough to put your faith in him. By all means examine him from every angle; search out the height and depth and length and breadth of his words and deeds. Compare him with others, if you wish. But be satisfied that Jesus is the Son of God, his words are words of life, his gospel, when lived, leads to true happiness. Delight in him. Worship him. Be devoted to him.

You heard Jesus say in Reading Twenty-four, "*Come to me*, all who labor and are burdened, and I will give you rest. Take my yoke upon you and *learn from me*." "Come to me... learn from me." All Christians should respond to this invitation wholeheartedly. We have gone to hear famous speakers, we have read books by popular authors, we have looked for advice from a variety of sources; yet the one person Christians should study under, first of all and above all, ought to be Jesus Christ himself. We should let his teachings form the basis for

our way of life. Let them be the solid foundation on which all our beliefs are built. Let them set the standard for our business practices. If other doctrines and principles do not agree with Jesus', let us have the good sense to stay away from them. Let us be wise enough to take a different route.

In Reading Twenty-five, Jesus reiterates the invitation to come to him: "Let anyone who is thirsty *come to me*! Let anyone who believes in me come and drink! As scripture says, 'From his heart shall flow streams of living water.'" From the heart of the person who goes to Jesus in faith the Holy Spirit can be poured out to give life abundantly.

"The kingdom of Heaven is like a mustard seed which a man took and sowed in his field. It is the smallest of all the seeds, but when it has grown it is the biggest of shrubs and becomes a tree, so that the birds of the air can come and shelter in its branches." When one allows the life of God to come in, the effect can far transcend its seemingly tiny beginning. Transformations will take place not only in him, but also in those who draw near.

In Reading Twenty-six, Jesus promises, "If you dwell in me, and my words dwell in you, ask what you want, and you shall have it." That is fantastic, isn't it? Make any request and it is granted! This will be possible when we dwell in Jesus and his words dwell in us. How can we dwell in him? "If you *heed my commands*, you will dwell in my love" (Jn 15:10, REB).

He goes on to say, "Anything you ask in my name, I will do, so that the Father may be glorified in the Son." This is a compelling reason for Jesus to answer our

prayers: that the Father be glorified. Therefore, go to Jesus for everything. Give him numerous occasions to heap praise and honour upon his Father.

He says, "Your Father knows what your needs are before you ask him." Just because God knows our needs does not mean we shouldn't talk to him about them. It is indeed proper to do so, for when we pour our hearts out to him in faith and simplicity, we put him at the centre of our being, we affirm our dependence on him, we acknowledge his ability to control the future. If we do not place our petitions before him and something good comes our way, we might be tempted to boast, "What good luck I have," or "I deserve this; I worked so hard for it." But if we do appeal to him and receive what is sought, we are more likely to say, "Thank you, God. Praise you." We will be glorifying our Father along with his Son.

Let us continue on this extremely important subject of prayer.

"At one place after Jesus had been praying, one of his disciples said, 'Lord, teach us to pray, as John taught his disciples.' He answered, 'When you pray, say, Father, may your name be hallowed; your kingdom come. Give us each day our daily bread. And forgive us our sins, for we too forgive all who have done us wrong. And do not put us to the test'" (Lk 11:1–4, REB). Jesus' reply meant, for one thing, that prayer should be God-centred and childlike. The goal of prayer is not the fancy things we can say or do. The mark of a person who prays well is not how much he thinks he knows about the topic. The mark of a person who prays well is the childlike trust he

puts in his heavenly Father. "In truth I tell, unless you change and become like little children you will never enter the kingdom of Heaven" (Mt 18:3, NJB). In saying this Jesus shows how we ought to relate to our Father and, consequently, the correct attitude to have when we pray.

Sometimes we may repeat short prayers like the Our Father. Doing this reflectively, in the prayer of meditation, does not constitute "babbling" or "heaping up empty phrases" (see Mt 6:7).

We should say formal prayers, but not mindlessly or just to get them over with. We should pray attentively and reverently, coming closer to God in friendship.

Prayer is not doing God a favour. Prayer is doing a favour for ourselves and for our neighbours. It is more beneficial to everyone if we pray with our hearts – purposefully and out of love – rather than grudgingly or hurriedly. It takes just as much time to pray politely as to pray rudely. Why not put in a bit of effort to concentrate on praying with courtesy? After all, we are speaking with our Creator.

The greatest prayer of the Church is the liturgy of the Holy Eucharist. Let us celebrate it consciously. Let us live it actively. Let it be for us an experience of God. If we are to pass judgment on the quality of a particular Sunday service, the criteria should not be the length of its duration, the calibre of the sermon, the choice of music by the choir, or whether other parishioners noticed us. If we are to evaluate, it should be done on the basis of the intensity of our own participation.

Pray and be exceedingly glad because prayer is a source of life for the whole world. Prayer makes the love of God present to his people. Those who are precious to you need your prayers. Those who are in trouble, including strangers, need your prayers. Imagine their gratitude when they find out eventually, in Heaven, that somewhere along the way it was your prayers and thoughtfulness that helped to call down divine assistance in their hour of need!

Through prayer we are united with God, we receive joy and peace, we obtain guidance and blessings. Through prayer we will have a way out of temptations. Through prayer we will be protected from sin.

Pray in the morning as you awaken; pray before and after your work; pray when you get ready for bed at night. Keep alive the spirit of prayer throughout the day, knowing that God loves you immensely.

If you have not been setting aside some time each day for the Lord, perhaps you can at least give him your spare moments while travelling in the car or bus, while standing in line, while awaiting your turn at the doctor's office or elsewhere, while walking alone, when you cannot fall asleep at night... Your life will not be boring, and you will do much good for yourself and for others.

To spend five minutes now and again with God in your heart, a very special place, is not a frivolous idea. It is possibly the beginning of the prayer of contemplation. Think about it, *contemplation*, as the word-origin indicates, means being with (*con*) God in a place set apart (*templum*).

As Jesus prayed frequently, so should we. As Jesus fasted, so should we. As he gave of himself for the good of humanity, so should we.

"When he saw the crowds, he had compassion for them, because they were harassed and helpless, like sheep without a shepherd. Then he said to his disciples, 'The harvest is plentiful, but the laborers are few; therefore ask the Lord of the harvest to send out laborers into his harvest'" (Mt 9:36–38, NRSV). Let us do as Jesus requests and offer this prayer to our Father. Let us go further and search ourselves to discover how we may, in one form or another, be an answer to the prayer.

Reading Twenty-seven contains three post-Resurrection narratives. "Now after he rose early on the first day of the week, he appeared first to Mary Magdalene." Mary received here a most wonderful sign of Jesus' affection. At his crucifixion she had remained loyal as the crowds turned against him. She did not run away while others fled. She believed in him even when many lost faith. If you wish to be special in Jesus' eyes, let your allegiance to him never falter.

Jesus also appeared to the disciples, by the Sea of Tiberias. You will recall that they had gone fishing all night but caught nothing. Just as they were about to give up, Jesus called out from the beach, "Cast the net to the right side of the boat, and you will find some." So they did and were rewarded with a huge catch. We, too, if we do what Jesus says, even if it seems impractical, will enjoy magnificent results in our undertakings – results beyond our wildest fantasy.

And when we have attained our heart's desires, when we have achieved our earthly goals, perhaps we will realize how insignificant they are after all. Like Peter, perhaps we will let go and turn our attention wholly to the Lord. "When Simon Peter heard it was the Lord he put on some clothes, for he was naked, and jumped into the sea" (Jn 21:7, NRSV). The fish and his success at catching them are no longer important. To come to Jesus, to be with him, to be his friend, that is important.

Notice that Peter did not beg to walk on the water this time. He swam ashore. His focus was on Jesus, not himself.

In this reading, Jesus asks, "Simon son of John, do you love me more than these?" If Jesus addresses the question to you, what would be your response?

The final reading, the twenty-eighth, is a brief summary. Jesus again urges: "Whoever loves me will keep my word, and my Father will love him, and we will come to him and make our dwelling with him. Whoever does not love me does not keep my words."

Watch the last sentence. A person's lack of love for Jesus is shown in his unwillingness to obey.

Jesus reminds us, "But seek first the kingdom of God and his righteousness." Seek first that God should be your king, that he reign over you, that his rules be the rules you live by. Seek first to rely on him as the benevolent king who looks out for your good, defends you, and provides for you. Seek first what he regards as righteous, not what unbelievers say it is. Seek first his very life. "And all these things will be *given* you besides."

Jesus loves you. Do you know how much? Do you know how much the Father loves Jesus? There is no love stronger than that which God the Father has for his Son. And yet that is exactly how much Jesus loves you! For he says: "As the Father loves me, so I also love you." In the same way! Just as profoundly. Just as tenderly. Just as limitlessly. Remain in his love. "If you *keep my commandments*, you will remain in my love."

Then, in the last line of this reading, we come to the closing verse of the Gospel according to Matthew. Jesus says, "And behold, I am with you always, until the end of the age." Keep that forever in your mind. Know without a doubt that Jesus is constantly present in you. He is present not only when you call upon him but even when you have forgotten him. Whether you feel neglected or restless, downcast or weary, he has not left you. At the times when you have problems, or when you doubt your own adequacy and worth, when you experience a sense of meaninglessness, when you feel unimportant and small, he remains near.

Moreover, "I am with you" also means "I am not against you! I am for you. Everything that I have ever done on earth has been for your sake. I created the world for you. I came to live, suffered, died, rose from the dead – all for you. Everything I have ever taught is for your good. Every word I have spoken is to bring you understanding and joy. Every commandment I have given is for your well-being.

"I am with you! I am by your side! I am on your side!"

Prayer

Jesus, Father, Holy Spirit,
you love your people.
You care deeply for them.
You want the finest for your children.
Your heart is always open to them.
And so you teach them with patience.
You prune them when they do not grow.
You look for them when they are lost.
You bring them back in the way they learn best.
Praise you, Lord.
Thank you for everything.

Reading Twenty-Five

Let anyone who is thirsty come to me! Let anyone who believes in me come and drink! As scripture says, "From his heart shall flow streams of living water."

The kingdom of Heaven is like a mustard seed which a man took and sowed in his field. It is the smallest of all the seeds, but when it has grown it is the biggest of shrubs and becomes a tree, so that the birds of the air can come and shelter in its branches.

This is what the kingdom of God is like. A man scatters seed on the land. Night and day, while he sleeps, when he is awake, the seed is sprouting and growing; how, he does not know. Of its own accord the land produces first the shoot, then the ear, then the full grain in the ear. And when the crop is ready, at once he starts to reap because the harvest has come.

It is to the glory of my Father that you should bear much fruit and be my disciples.

1. Jn 7:37–38. 2. Mt 13:31–32. 3. Mk 4:26–29. 4. Jn 15:8. (NJB)

*

Reading Twenty-Six

If you dwell in me, and my words dwell in you, ask what you want, and you shall have it.

Anything you ask in my name I will do, so that the Father may be glorified in the Son. If you ask anything in my name I will do it.

Ask, and you will receive; seek, and you will find; knock, and the door will be opened to you. For everyone who asks receives, those who seek find, and to those who knock, the door will be opened.

Is there a man among you who will offer his son a stone when he asks for bread, or a snake when he asks for fish? If you, then, bad as you are, know how to give your children what is good for them, how much more will your heavenly Father give good things to those who ask him!

I tell you, then, whatever you ask for in prayer, believe that you have received it and it will be yours.

Again, when you pray, do not be like the hypocrites; they love to say their prayers standing up in synagogues and at street corners for everyone to see them. Truly I tell you: they have their reward already. But when you pray, go into a room by yourself, shut the door and pray to your Father who is in secret; and your Father who sees what is done in secret will reward you.

In your prayers do not go babbling on like the heathen, who imagine that the more they say the more likely they are to be heard. Do not imitate them, for your Father knows what your needs are before you ask him.

When you pray, say, "Father, may your name be hallowed; your kingdom come. Give us each day our daily bread. And forgive us our sins, for we too forgive all who have done us wrong. And do not put us to the test."

1. Jn 15:7. 2. Jn 14:13–14. 3. Mt 7:7–11. 4. Mk 11:24. 5. Mt 6:5–8. 6. Lk 11:2–4. (REB)

*

Reading Twenty-Seven

Now after he rose early on the first day of the week, he appeared first to Mary Magdalene, from whom he had cast out seven demons.

After these things Jesus showed himself again to the disciples by the Sea of Tiberias; and he showed himself in this way. Gathered there together were Simon Peter, Thomas called the Twin, Nathanael of Cana in Galilee, the sons of Zebedee, and two others of his disciples. Simon Peter said to them, "I am going fishing." They said to him, "We will go with you." They went out and got into the boat, but that night they caught nothing.

Jesus said to them, "Children, you have no fish, have you?" They answered him, "No." He said to them, "Cast the net to the right side of the boat, and you will find some." So they cast it, and now they were not able to haul it in because there were so many fish.

Jesus said to them, "Come and have breakfast."

When they had finished breakfast, Jesus said to Simon Peter, "Simon son of John, do you love me more than these?" He said to him, "Yes, Lord: you know that I love you." Jesus said to him, "Feed my lambs."

Then he opened their minds to understand the scriptures, and said to them, "Thus it is written, that the Messiah is to suffer and to rise from the dead on the third day, and that repentance and forgiveness of sins is to be proclaimed in his name to all nations, beginning from Jerusalem. You are witnesses of these things. And see, I am sending upon you what my Father promised; so stay here in the city until you have been clothed with power from on high."

Then he led them out as far as Bethany, and, lifting up his hands, he blessed them. While he was blessing them, he withdrew from them and was carried up into heaven. And they worshipped him, and returned to Jerusalem with great joy; and they were continually in the temple blessing God.

1. Mk 16:9. 2. Jn 21:1–3. 3. Jn 21:5–6. 4. Jn 21:12. 5. Jn 21:15. 6. Lk 24:45–53. (NRSV)

*

Reading Twenty-Eight

You shall love the Lord, your God, with all your heart, with all your soul, and with all your mind. This is the greatest and the first commandment. The second is like it: You shall love your neighbor as yourself. The whole law and the prophets depend on these two commandments.

Whoever loves me will keep my word, and my Father will love him, and we will come to him and make our dwelling with him. Whoever does not love me does not keep my words.

I came into the world as light, so that everyone who believes in me might not remain in darkness. And if anyone hears my words and does not observe them, I do not condemn him, for I did not come to condemn the world but to save the world. Whoever rejects me and does not accept my words has something to judge him: the word that I spoke, it will condemn him on the last day.

As the Father loves me, so I also love you. Remain in my love. If you keep my commandments, you will remain in my love, just as I have kept my Father's commandments and remain in his love.

I have told you this so that my joy might be in you and your joy might be complete. This is my commandment: love one another as I love you. No one has greater love than this, to lay down one's life for one's friends. You are my friends if you do what I command you.

So do not worry and say, "What are we to eat?" or "What are we to drink?" or "What are we to wear?" All these things the pagans seek. Your heavenly Father knows that you need them all. But seek first the kingdom of God and his righteousness, and all these things will be given you besides.

I have told you this while I am with you. The Advocate, the holy Spirit that the Father will send in my name – he will teach you everything and remind you of all that I told you. Peace I leave with you; my peace I give to you. Not as the world gives do I give it to you. Do not let your hearts be troubled or afraid.

And behold, I am with you always, until the end of the age.

1. Mt 22:37–40. 2. Jn 14:23–24. 3. Jn 12:46–48. 4. Jn 15:9–14. 5. Mt 6:31–33. 6. Jn 14:25–27. 7. Mt 28:20. (NAB)

AN EXERCISE

Consider this question: How has living the gospel more attentively affected my attitudes and behaviour lately towards the following? Use as reference points the fruits of the Holy Spirit: love, joy, peace, patience, kindness, generosity, fidelity, gentleness, and self-control.

my spouse
my children
my parents
my other relatives
my friends
my fellow workers
the poor – in material possessions
          – in intelligence
          – in education
          – in looks
          – in sophistication
          – in personality
          – in efficiency
          – in emotional and/or physical health
myself
money
social status
fear of unbelievers' ridicule
my faith in Jesus' way
God

JESUS

We now wind up with three central aspects of Christian life – companionship with Jesus, promulgation of his teachings, and Holy Communion.

First. A key principle of spiritual priorities can be seen in this passage: "He now went up onto the mountain and summoned those he wanted. So they came to him and he appointed twelve; they were to be his companions and to be sent out to proclaim the message, with power to drive out devils" (Mk 3:13–15, NJB). Wherein lies the special significance of the passage? It lies in the order of importance Jesus places on the following: before he dispatched his apostles to preach and cast out evil spirits, he appointed them first of all *to be his companions*. When he calls us, it is first and foremost for the same purpose: to be his companions, to be with him.

How do we become Jesus' companions? How do we become his friends? He said, "You are my friends, if you do what I command you" (Jn 15:14, REB). The requirement is undeviating: keep his commandments!

Many of us yearn to serve God in some way. Many of us long to do something of value for him. These are normal aspirations. But it should be noted that, to Jesus, service does not mean extraordinary exploits. The tasks he has in mind are those he exemplified in the washing of his apostles' feet at the Last Supper. We please God

by ministering to our neighbours in small kindnesses, not by driving out demons or performing other phenomenal feats. "Nevertheless, do not rejoice because the spirits are subject to you, but rejoice because your names are written in heaven" (Lk 10:20, NAB).

There may be occasions, once in a while, when he does give us a tiny extra assignment. But that is his decision. It is his choice. We have to await his order.

Jesus waited (see Lk 2:51–52). John the Baptist waited (see Lk 1:80). Even after the disciples walked with Jesus for three years, they were made to wait longer. Before Jesus ascended into heaven he told them, "And see, I am sending upon you what my Father promised; so stay here in the city until you have been clothed with power from on high" (Lk 24:49, NRSV). They had to wait for the descent of the Holy Spirit. They had to stay in Jerusalem. They did not know for how long.

And this was how they waited. They "returned to Jerusalem full of joy, and spent all their time in the temple praising God" (Lk 24:52–53, REB). They waited with joy. They praised God continually. They remained in the temple, not going off in their own directions. That is how we ought to spend our days. Let the Holy Spirit determine when to clothe us with his power for any additional mission he chooses for us. In the meantime, we must not allow boredom and depression to enter. Let us occupy ourselves with what is joyful and constructive, remembering Jesus' words, "Many who are first will be last, and the last, first" (Mt 19:30, NJB).

To wait upon the Lord with joy and patience requires great love. To wait upon the Lord with joy and patience

is loving him greatly. And patience is less difficult to acquire if we understand that time seems to creep along very slowly only when we look ahead into the future. If we look back instead, we can see that years and years have gone by in the twinkling of an eye. Therefore, do not anticipate the next 'big' event by counting the hours; do not sit around and let the present crawl sluggishly by. Do cheerfully what is there to do today, help the person who needs you, arrange some recreation, pray, become more and more a friend of Jesus, and tomorrow will arrive just as quickly as yesterday went by.

Second. When Jesus gave the apostles their ministry, what did he intend them to preach? Examine Mark 3:14 again, this time in the *Revised English Bible*. "He appointed twelve to be his companions, and to be sent out to proclaim *the gospel*." The gospel, that was what they were to preach. Luke recorded the following when, earlier, Jesus had ordered his disciples to go forth, permitting them a foretaste of their up-coming duties: "So they set out and went from village to village proclaiming *the good news*" (Lk 9:6, NJB). The "good news," that is, Jesus' gospel. In Matthew 28:18–20 (NRSV), Jesus issued this great commission: "All authority in heaven and on earth has been given to me. Go therefore and make disciples of all nations, baptizing them in the name of the Father and of the Son and of the Holy Spirit, and teaching them to obey *everything that I have commanded you*."

In the same way, the apostles of today are asked to teach what Jesus commanded. They are to spread his

gospel everywhere, urging his people to come to him, exhorting them to learn from him.

"Jesus had now finished what he wanted to say, and his teaching made a deep impression on the people because he taught them with authority, unlike their own scribes" (Mt 7:28–29, NJB). "His teaching," what he considers important, makes deep impressions on people. It affects those who hear. It leaves lasting imprints on their hearts and minds. If Jesus sends us out, let us be sure to promulgate his words. Let us promote his messages. Let us stress what he stresses. His power accompanies his commands. All authority has been given to him, both in heaven and on earth.

"This is what the kingdom of God is like. A man scatters seed on the land. Night and day, while he sleeps, when he is awake, the seed is sprouting and growing; how, he does not know. Of its own accord the land produces first the shoot, then the ear, then the full grain in the ear. And when the crop is ready, at once he starts to reap because the harvest has come" (Mk 4:26–29, NJB). When the words of Jesus are sown into receptive hearts, they will germinate and take root. We do not have to worry about the results. The gospel will do its appointed work. You can be sure of that.

So, let us raise up Jesus' teachings. "What I say to you in the dark, tell in the daylight; what you hear in whispers, proclaim from the housetops" (Mt 10:27, NJB). "And just as Moses lifted up the serpent in the wilderness, so must the Son of Man be lifted up, that whoever believes in him may have eternal life" (Jn 3:14–15, NRSV). "And I, when I am lifted up from the

earth, will draw all people to myself" (Jn 12:32, NRSV). Jesus is the one to be elevated, not someone else. When that is done, he will draw his people. And he will draw them, not to any other human being, but to himself. That is as it should be.

Third. Before discussing the next point, let us learn from the woman who showered her love on Jesus without being coerced. She earned her place in the gospel. "When he was in Bethany reclining at table in the house of Simon the leper, a woman came with an alabaster jar of perfumed oil, costly genuine spikenard. She broke the alabaster jar and poured it on his head. There were some who were indignant. 'Why has there been this waste of perfumed oil? It could have been sold for more than three hundred days' wages and the money given to the poor.' They were infuriated with her. Jesus said, 'Let her alone. Why do you make trouble for her? She has done a good thing for me. The poor you will always have with you, and whenever you wish you can do good to them, but you will not always have me. She has done what she could. She has anticipated anointing my body for burial. Amen, I say to you, wherever the gospel is proclaimed to the whole world, what she has done will be told in memory of her'" (Mk 14:3–9, NAB). This woman did not have to give the perfume to Jesus. No one was compelling her to do so. Yet she did it gratuitously, despite much criticism, and with considerable extravagance.

We, too, can be extravagant to Jesus by voluntarily doing all that he requests in the gospel, and not just coasting along with the bare minimum. We can devote

more attention to him – especially in prayer – and a little less to small talk, eating and drinking, shopping, music, television, magazines, games, sports, and other forms of amusement. We can lead more holy lives, giving increased quiet time to listening to the voice of the Holy Spirit, worshipping and thanking God, interceding for sinners and unbelievers and offering penance on their behalf. We can lay down our lives for our sons and daughters, for our husbands or wives, relatives, friends, God's other children, and for his Church.

Now, as Jesus was gracious to the woman at Bethany, so is he gracious to us: he has given us an additional way to become his companions. Without going into any depth, we conclude this book by mentioning it.

The term *companion* is a composite of the prefix *com* and the Latin *panis*. *Com* means 'with' and *panis* means 'bread.' A companion is one who shares bread with you. When Jesus shares bread, he shares himself, for he says, "I am the bread of life... The bread which I shall give is my own flesh... Whoever eats my flesh and drinks my blood dwells in me and I in him" (Jn 6:48, 51, 56, REB). This is Holy Communion. When we partake of the Sacred Bread we become Jesus' friends in the closest interrelationship – we live continually in him, and he in us.

Holy Communion is not just something nice to do. It is vital. Jesus says, "In very truth I tell you, unless you eat the flesh of the Son of Man and drink his blood you can have no *life* in you." It is that vital. Conversely, "Whoever eats my flesh and drinks my blood has *eternal life*" (Jn 6:53, 54, REB). Beginning this instant!

What do 'life' and 'eternal life' mean in the above context? Each kind of being has its own distinctive type of life or existence. God has God-life, the angels have angelic-life, and humans have human-life. These are followed by animal-life, plant-life, and inanimate existence. In the Gospels according to Mark, Matthew, and Luke, God's life is often referred to as *the kingdom of God*, or *the reign of God*, or *the kingdom of Heaven*. We have come across these expressions several times. In the Gospel according to John, the terms employed to denote God-life are simply *life* and *eternal life*. When we receive Holy Communion, God's life comes into us. "As the living Father sent me and I draw *life* from the Father, so whoever eats me will also draw *life* from me" (Jn 6:57, NJB).

Holy Communion is life-giving. What should we do about it? Two things. Both are requested by Jesus. Number one: "Now as they were eating, Jesus took bread, and blessed, and broke it, and gave it to the disciples and said, 'Take, eat; this is my body'" (Mt 26:26, NRSV). In other words, go to Holy Communion. Take, eat! And perhaps we might go not only on Sundays, but on some weekdays as well, not as an obligation but as a way of nurturing our friendship with Jesus. We can be extravagant in this way.

Number two: "Then he took bread, and when he had given thanks, he broke it and gave it to them, saying, 'This is my body given for you; do this in remembrance of me'" (Lk 22:19, NJB). Remember him! Remember him! Do not go to Communion as a matter of routine. Do not take Jesus for granted. Bring him to mind over and

over again. Let him be the object and centre of your attention. Let his life be reinforced in you.

Remembrance of Jesus is an outstanding prayer. No word needs to be spoken. He has said, "And look, I am with you always" (Mt 28:20, NJB). This is one promise you must never forget. Believe it with all your might. Jesus is truly present. He is close to you. He knows your problems and takes care of you. Trust him. Trust his love. Trust his providence. When you turn habitually to him and away from yourself, you will begin to experience the peace he promised. "I am the bread of life; whoever comes to me will never hunger, and whoever believes in me will never thirst" (Jn 6:35, NAB). There will be no more pining and craving, no more hungering and thirsting. A peace that surpasses all understanding will descend upon you. There will be quiet joy.

Keep remembering Jesus and you will soon discover that he himself continually remembers you. He never takes you for granted. He is always bringing you to mind, putting you at the centre of his attention. Again and again he proves to be the one who does not forget. He is the extravagant friend, he is the true companion. He it is who, day after day, longs to share bread with you. He it is who, time and time again, hungers and thirsts to give you his very own life.

"Then many of his disciples who were listening said, 'This saying is hard; who can accept it?' Since Jesus knew that his disciples were murmuring about this, he said to them, 'Does this shock you? What if you were to

see the Son of Man ascending to where he was before? It is the spirit that gives life, while the flesh is of no avail. The words I have spoken to you are spirit and life. But there are some of you who do not believe.' Jesus knew from the beginning the ones who would not believe and the one who would betray him. And he said, 'For this reason I have told you that no one can come to me unless it is granted him by my Father.'

"As a result of this, many of his disciples returned to their former way of life and no longer accompanied him. Jesus then said to the Twelve, 'Do you also want to leave?' Simon Peter answered him, 'Master, to whom shall we go? You have the words of eternal life. We have come to believe and are convinced that you are the Holy One of God.' Jesus answered them, 'Did I not choose you twelve? Yet is not one of you a devil?' He was referring to Judas, son of Simon the Iscariot; it was he who would betray him, one of the Twelve" (Jn 6:60–71, NAB).

FINAL WORDS

Be sure to read from the Gospels every day. Open your heart and ears to Jesus. Listen to him; do whatever he tells you.

Keep in mind his explanation of the parable of the sower and the seed.

The sower sows the word. With some the seed falls along the footpath; no sooner have they heard it than Satan comes and carries off the word which has been sown in them. With others the seed falls on rocky ground; as soon as they hear the word, they accept it with joy, but it strikes no root in them; they have no staying-power, and when there is trouble or persecution on account of the word, they quickly lose faith. With others again the seed falls among thistles; they hear the word, but worldly cares and the false glamour of wealth and evil desires of all kinds come in and choke the word, and it proves barren. But there are some with whom the seed is sown on good soil; they accept the word when they hear it, and they bear fruit thirtyfold, sixtyfold, or a hundredfold.

(Mk 4:14-20, REB)

The Ave Maria Centre of Peace
P.O. Box 498, Station U
Toronto, Ontario, M8Z 5Y8
Canada

Tel.: 416-251-4245
Fax: 416-253-0480
E-mail: letters@avemaria.ca

Parts of any book can be easily misinterpreted due to inaccuracy of quotation and reading out of context. Do exercise the greatest care.

Permission must be obtained from the author, or his heirs, before translation is allowed.

Note that because the citations used here are from Bibles published in England and the United States, some spellings will be British, and some American.

A note to translators of this book

The Gospels were written many centuries ago in an ancient tongue. It is impossible for one English version of these sacred texts to bring out completely and exactly what was in the minds of the inspired evangelists. That is why the quotations in *Do Whatever Jesus Tells You!* are taken from four different editions of the holy books. Two of these have been prepared by Catholics, and the others by Protestants. All of them are the result of years of intense research and collaboration carried out by broadly representative panels of experts in Scripture, linguistics, theology, history, and other related fields. To accomplish their task, these professionals employed the highest standards of scholarship, using the best and oldest extant manuscripts of the Bible.

Translators of this book are advised to likewise consult at least two responsible and authoritative renditions of the New Testament.

It has taken more than 33 years to complete this book. Please translate faithfully and prayerfully. There must be no additions, subtractions, or alterations. Words and ideas must not be injected into the material to conform to the thoughts of current popular writers and speakers.

Access to a large comprehensive dual-language dictionary is mandatory, as well as a thesaurus of synonyms.

ii

Acknowledgments

In this work, citations followed by the letters NAB are excerpts taken from the *NEW AMERICAN BIBLE WITH REVISED NEW TESTAMENT* copyright © 1990 by the Confraternity of Christian Doctrine, Washington, D.C. and are used with permission. All rights reserved.

The initials NRSV indicate that the Scripture quotations are from the *NEW REVISED STANDARD VERSION BIBLE:* Catholic Edition, copyright 1989, 1993, Division of Christian Education of the National Council of the Churches of Christ in the United States of America. Used by permission. All rights reserved.

Any passage designated NJB is an excerpt from *THE NEW JERUSALEM BIBLE*, copyright © 1990 by Darton, Longman & Todd, Ltd. and Doubleday, a division of Random House, Inc. Reprinted by permission.

Texts marked REB are from the *REVISED ENGLISH BIBLE* © Oxford University Press and Cambridge University Press 1989.

National Library of Canada Cataloguing in Publication Data

Yeung, Andrew Jerome, 1938 –
    Do whatever Jesus tells you!

Previous eds. published under title: Live Jesus' Gospel, Now!

ISBN 0-9693729-1-4

    1. Jesus Christ – Words. 2. Jesus Christ – Teachings. 3. Christian life – Catholic authors. I. Ave Maria Centre of Peace. II. Yeung, Andrew Jerome, 1938–. Live Jesus' Gospel, Now! III. Title.

BT306.Y48 2004   232.9'54   C2002-9010225

Ave Maria Centre of Peace
P.O. Box 498, Station U
Toronto ON M8Z 5Y8
Canada

Printed and bound in Canada.

Do Whatever Jesus Tells You!

Second edition

ANDREW JEROME YEUNG

Published by
Ave Maria Centre of Peace
Toronto, Canada

Do Wh ⟡ W9-BBU-371
Jesus
Tells You!

ANDREW JEROME
YEUNG